DEATH IS OF VITAL IMPORTANCE

DEATH IS OF VITAL IMPORTANCE

On Life, Death and Life After Death

ELISABETH KÜBLER-ROSS, M.D.

Compiled and Edited by Göran Grip, M.D.
Photographs by Ken Ross

STATION HILL PRESS

Published by Station Hill Press, Inc., Barrytown, New York 12507.

Distributed by the Talman Company, 131 Spring Street, Suite 201 E-N, New York, New York 10012.

Photographs by Ken Ross, on the cover and throughout this book, are used by permission of the photographer.

Text and cover design by Susan Quasha.

A Swedish version of this book has been published by Bokförlaget Natur och Kultur under the title *Döden är livsviktig: Om livet, döden och livet efter döden*, Copyright 1991 by Elisabeth Kübler-Ross.

Grateful acknowledgement is due to Celestial Arts, a subsidiary of Ten Speed Press, of Box 7327, Berkeley, California 94707, for permission to reprint, in a differently edited form newly transcribed from the original taped lecture, the piece, "Life, Death, and Life After Death," from the book, *On Life After Death* (Copyright 1991 by Elisabeth Kübler-Ross). All English language rights reserved.

Library of Congress Cataloging-in-Publication Data

Kübler-Ross, Elisabeth.
       Death is of vital importance : on life, death, and life after
death / Elisabeth Kübler-Ross ; compiled and edited by Göran Grip.
       p.   cm.
       ISBN 0-88268-186-9 : $12.95
       1. Death. 2. Life. 3. Future Life. 4. Spiritual life.
5. Kübler-Ross, Elisabeth.   I. Grip, Göran.   II. Title.
BD444.K79   1995
155.9'37—dc20

                    95—5850
                    CIP

Manufactured in the United States of America

Contents

About This Book   *vii*

Editor's Foreword   *ix*

DEATH IS OF VITAL IMPORTANCE   1
(First Stockholm Lecture, 1980)

Maidanek   2

The Symbolic Language   6

Children Losing a Relative   10

Jamie's Brother   11

Lorrie   12

The Boy in San Diego   19

Interpretation of Children's Drawings   20

Liz   24

Dougy   29

The Meaning of Suffering   34

THE COCOON AND THE BUTTERFLY   41
(Second Stockholm Lecture, 1981)

The Four Quadrants   42

The Five Natural Emotions   49

Billy   53

Jeffy   56

The Near Death Experience   68

The Common Denominators   71

LIFE, DEATH AND LIFE AFTER DEATH   79
(1980)

Mrs. Schwartz   80

You Cannot Die Alone   83

Susie   84

Children Seeing Dead Relatives   86

The Indian Woman   87

The Bum   89

Peter   91
Corry   92
The Tunnel and the Light   93
The Life Review   94
Mrs. Schwartz's Visit   95
One of My First Mystical Experiences   98
To Say Yes to It   100
Cosmic Consciousness   104

HEALING IN OUR TIME   109
    (Washington, 1982)
The Paralyzed Woman   111
The Black Cleaning Woman   114
The Schnook   117
Bernie Siegel   125
Chemotherapy   126
The Gnomes   128
The Workshops   129
Christ   130
Dougy Again   132

TO SAY YES TO IT   137
    (The Edgar Cayce Foundation, Virginia Beach, 1985)
Good Friday   137
Suicide Out of Free Choice   140
Suicide as a Result of an Endogenous Depression   141
The Difference Between Rescue and Help   142
My Mother   144
My Father   152
Diagnosing Black Bunnies   159

Publisher's Afterword   161
About the Author, About the Editor   164

About This Book

Elisabeth Kübler-Ross' words, spoken at the spur of the moment, have been edited here with the aim of creating a readable text. We have taken pains, however, to preserve the quality of immediate presence that is characterized by the author's special magnetism, the power of direct address to actual people in a room for which she is renowned. We think there is a special meaning in presenting Elisabeth Kübler-Ross "live" on the subject of death and dying — and that this is a key to her message.

There are in these chapters inevitable differences from the "original": for instance, various versions of the same story, told on different occasions, have been edited together into a more nearly definitive version, placed in context according the logic of reading. Particular sections have been moved from one lecture to another in order to avoid unnecessary diversion and to give the reader a line of thought to follow. Nothing essential has been changed, however, and hardly anything from the tapes is omitted.

The book is compiled from the following tape recordings of lectures given by Elisabeth Kübler-Ross:

Death Does not Exist, 1976

Life, Death and Life After Death, 1980

Death Is of Vital Importance, Stockholm, Sweden, 1980

"(Second lecture)," Stockholm, Sweden, 1981

Healing in Our Time, Washington, 1982

The ARE Lecture (at the Edgar Cayce Foundation), Virginia Beach, Virginia, 1985

Making the Most of the Inbetween, 1987

The Tucson Workshop (private recording), Tucson, Arizona, 1989

Elisabeth Kübler-Ross on farm

Editor's Foreword

Dear Elisabeth,

This is in my opinion your best book so far. For years I have in vain been looking for something like it in book stores both here in Sweden and abroad.

I remember the day when I started looking for it. I was a young doctor and by chance (or rather by "chance") I came across a magazine article where you told a story about a young girl, Liz, who was dying of cancer. But Liz couldn't die because there was something that scared her and held her back.

I will never forget the revelation I felt when I read how you helped her to finish her unfinished business. You taught me that it was possible to help her without having to attack those who had scared her in the first place. In a flash I realized something that I had never been taught during my medical training: you can use the patient's own inner resources and life experiences to help her cope successfully with difficult life situations.

I wanted to read more of this. I wanted to find the book where you had collected all those wonderful, touching, powerful stories of victory: mind over matter, spirit over body, love over fear and guilt.

I also wanted to read about your findings on the near death experience and other spiritual experiences. And I wanted to read about your life. Not out of curiosity of course, but because there is always a lesson to be learned in finding out what made a pioneer into a pioneer. What were the questions of your childhood to which your life's work is an answer? Once I knew those questions I would be able to see the answer – your life work – more clearly.

But I never found that book. And that's because it didn't exist, although later on *On Children and Death* came close to it. And so I gave up my hopes that you would ever write it.

One day a couple of months ago my Swedish publisher asked me to translate two of your tape recorded lectures into Swedish. A quick job, he said. And there it was again: Liz's story! The story that I now knew had given direction to my own work as a care giver. Suddenly I also remembered another one of your stories, the one about Jeffy, who wanted... well I don't want to reveal that in advance to the reader.

Anyway I wanted to add that story to the manuscript and asked a friend for the cassette tape where you told it. By "chance" she sent me the wrong tape, where I found even more of these powerful stories and also a lot on the near death experience.

By "chance" I also met a friend who was just about to go to Virginia to see you. I asked her to buy me a certain tape from *Shanti Nilaya*. She didn't, but instead she brought me another five tapes with more on your own spiritual experiences and some very touching and insightful stories from your own childhood and family, stories shedding an unveiling light on the very words with which you opened your first lecture in Stockholm in 1980: *thrifty... authoritarian... unliberal...*, the lecture which has now become the first chapter of this book.

Those stories tell me once again that anything – just *anything* – can be turned into love and service for others.

And so, thanks to Comrade "Chance" (or divine manipulation, as I know you yourself would call it), I suddenly found myself typing, editing, compiling that very book by you, which I had been eagerly looking for for so many years! What a surprise!

And here it is, Elisabeth, your best book so far! Five powerful lessons for your intuition!

And your readers don't have to be doctors to enjoy them. They don't have to have *any* formal education to learn from them. The only thing they need is to have graduated from Primary School of Intuition, and to be ready to learn by example rather than from theories, and that you are willing to grow as a care giver, as a helper and as a human being.

And thanks, Elisabeth, for giving me, the editor, this opportunity to come close to your teaching, to your experiences and thoughts, and – in a way – to your life.

With lots of love,
Göran Grip, M.D.
Uppsala, Sweden
July 1989

P.S., September 1991:

Shortly after having finished the manuscript of this book I was given a biography about you called *Quest,* written by journalist Derek Gill. In an epilogue you explain why that book only included your life through 1969. And then you go on to write: 'I believe this book [i.e., *Quest*] will be seen as even more significant when the story of my later years, and of our research into life after death, is published in the future, and it is seen why that which happened to me *had* to happen.'

And then you go on to describe the very book that I unknowingly compiled for you here in Sweden eight years later!

Reading this made me think of the many discussions I had with my editor as our translation project little by little grew into something much greater: with a laugh she said that obviously this book *wanted* to come into existence, and that we only had to obey what it told us to do. She was right. This book *did* want to come into existence. It was already planned for. And I was the one who got the privilege of doing the job.

Elisabeth Kübler-Ross with Erika and Eva (the triplets, 1976)

DEATH IS OF VITAL IMPORTANCE

I was born in Switzerland in a typically Swiss family, very thrifty like most Swiss, very authoritarian like most Swiss, very ... unliberal, if you can say that. We had all the material things in the world and we had loving parents.

But I was born an "unwanted" child. Not that my parents didn't want a child. They wanted a girl very badly, but a pretty, beautiful, ten-pound girl. They did not expect triplets and when I came, I was only two pounds. I was very ugly and had no hair, and I was a terribly, terribly big disappointment to my parents.

Fifteen minutes later the second one came, and after another twenty minutes a six and a half pound baby came, and *then* they were very happy. But they would have liked to give two of us back.

So I had the tragedy of being born a triplet. That is the biggest tragedy, that I don't wish my worst enemy. If you are raised an identical triplet, it is very peculiar because you can literally drop dead and nobody would know the difference. I had the feeling that I had to prove all my life that even I, a two-pound nothing, was worth something. I had to work really hard for that, in the same way that some blind people think that they have to work ten times as hard as everybody else in order to keep their job. I had to prove very hard that I was worth living.

I had to be born and raised in this way in order to do this work. It took me fifty years to understand that. It took me fifty years to realize that there are no coincidences in life, not even the circumstances of our birth, and that the things we regard as tragedies are not really tragedies unless we choose to make tragedies out of them. Because we can also choose to regard them as chances for us, opportunities to grow, and then we see that they are challenges and hints that we may need to change our lives.

When you are at the end of your life and look back, not at the easy days but at the tough days, at the windstorms of life, you see that the tough days are the ones that really made you what you are today. It is like ... somebody said once, "It's like putting a rock in a tumbler. You have the choice to come out crashed or polished."

And to be raised as a triplet is such a challenge: for years and years and years knowing, being totally aware of the fact that my own mother and father didn't know whether they talked to me or to my sister, being aware that my teachers didn't know whether I deserved an A or an F, and therefore always gave us C's.

One day my sister went on her first date. She was in love like a typical teenager who is in love for the first time. The second time the boy invited her she became very sick and just couldn't go and was heartbroken. Then I said to her, "don't worry. If you really can't go and you are heartbroken and afraid that you are going to lose him, I will go for you. *(amusement from audience)* And he will never know the difference."

I asked her how far she went. And I went on the date for her, and her boyfriend never noticed the difference. *(amusement from audience)*

You may think now, looking back, that it's a funny story, but for a teenager like me it was very tragic to think that you could be in love with somebody, that you could go out with him, and that you were *totally* and completely and absolutely replaceable. Sometimes I even wonder if I am not my sister.

I needed to learn this lesson early in life, because after this incident, when I realized that my sister's boyfriend didn't know the difference between her and me, I probably made the most difficult choice in my whole life and that was to leave Switzerland, to leave my family, to leave the security of my home. I went on a trip through post war Europe. I also came to Sweden where I gave a workshop for workshop leaders.

Maidanek

I ended up in Maidanek in Poland, in a concentration camp where I saw train loads of baby shoes of murdered children, train loads of human hair. To read about this in books is one thing, but to stand there and see the crematories and smell it with your own nose is something quite different.

I was nineteen and I came from a country where there are no windstorms. We have no race problem, no poverty, and we have had no war for 760 years. I didn't know what life was. In this place, suddenly all the windstorms of life came flooding down on me. After an experience like that, one will never ever be the same person again. And I bless this day. Without that windstorm I would not be in this work today.

I asked myself: how can grownups, men and women like you and I, kill 960,000 innocent children and at the same time worry about their own children at home having chicken-pox?

And then I went to the barracks where the children had spent the last night of their life, not knowing why but, I guess, in search of messages or cues how these children had faced death. The children had scratched symbols into the barrack walls with their finger nails or a piece of rock or chalk, and the most frequent one of them were butterflies.

I saw those butterflies. I was very young. I was very ignorant. I had no idea why five, six, seven, eight, nine-year-old children who were taken away from home, from their parents, from the security of their homes and schools into cattle cars, and shipped to Auschwitz and Buchenwald and Maidanek, why these children should see butterflies. It took me a quarter of a century to find the answer.

Maidanek was the beginning of my work.

In Maidanek I found a young Jewish girl who stayed there instead of leaving. I couldn't understand why. She had lost her grandparents, her parents and all her brothers and sisters in the gas chamber in the concentration camp. The gas chamber had been filled and then they couldn't squeeze another person into it, and so she was spared.

In my horror I asked her, "What in the world are you doing here. Why do you stay here in this place of inhumanity?" She said, "during the last few weeks of the concentration camp I swore to myself that I was going to survive to do nothing but tell the world of all the horrors of the Nazis and the concentration camps. Then the liberation army came. I looked at those people and I said to myself: 'No. If I would do that, I would be no better than Hitler himself.' Because what else would I then do but to plant even more seeds of hate and negativity in the world? But if I can truly believe that no-body gets more than they can take, that we are never alone, that I can acknowledge the tragedy and the nightmare of Maidanek and leave it behind, if I can touch one single human life and turn it away from negativity, from hate, from revenge, from bitterness into one that who can serve and love and care, then it may be worthwhile and I deserved to survive."

Negativity can only feed on negativity and will then continue to grow like a cancer grows. But we also have the choice to accept what happened as a sad and horrible reality, which is gone, which has passed, and which she cannot be changed. And she made that choice.

What she *could* change, however, was what she was going to do, what she was going to make out of all that had happened. And so she decided to stay in this horrible place of horrible sights and smells.

She and I went to the barracks. She and I discovered the butter-flies. She and I began to talk like two young people. She and I began to philosophize together about life and death. And she was the one who said to me, "don't you believe, Elisabeth, that in all of us there is a Hitler?" She and I realized at a very young age that it *really* depends only on our own courage to look at our own negativity and our own negative potential, if we are to become serving, loving human beings. Because in all of us there is *also* the potential of be-coming a Mother Theresa.

We parted ways. I went back to Switzerland. I studied medicine. My dream was to go somewhere in Africa or India and become a doctor like Albert Schweitzer. But two weeks before I was supposed to leave for India, I was notified that the whole project there had fallen through. And instead of the jungles of India I ended up in the jungles of Brooklyn, New York. I married an American, who took me to the one place in the world that was at the bottom of my list of places where I ever wanted to live: New York City, the biggest jungle in the world. I was *very* unhappy.

As a foreign doctor in New York it is impossible to find a good residency in June, and so I ended up in a Manhattan State Hospital with chronic, hopeless, schizophrenic patients. I had trouble under-standing their English. When they talked Schizophrenese to me they could as well have been talking Chinese. I didn't know any psy-chiatry. I was a good country doctor but I was not a psychiatrist.

Not really knowing any psychiatry, and being very lonely and miserable and unhappy, and not wanting to make my new husband unhappy, I opened up to the patients. I identified with their misery and their loneliness and their desperation.

And suddenly my patients started to talk. People who hadn't talked for twenty years started to verbalize and share their feelings. Suddenly I knew that I was not alone in my misery, though *m y* mis-ery wasn't half as bad as living in a state hospital. For two years I did nothing but live and work with these patients, sharing every Hanukkah, Christmas, Passover and Easter with them, just to share their loneliness, not knowing much psychiatry, the theoretical psy-chiatry that one ought to know. I barely understood their English, but we loved each other. We really cared.

I began to listen to them. Not to their language but to their non-verbal, symbolic communications. Then I realized that the only thing that turned those people on, that made them behave and react like human beings, were two things, both of them very unhealthy but all the same very human. It was cigarettes and Coca Cola.

Only when they received cigarettes and Coke did they show any human reactions and responses. Many of them had been in the state hospital locked up worse than animals for up to twenty years.

And so I did. Again, I had to make a choice. I took the cigarettes and the Coke away from them. That was very hard for me, because I am a softy. I told them that if they wanted to learn self respect and regain some degree of dignity and self-worth and become human again, they had to *earn* their benefits.

And in one week those people, who really didn't respond to any-thing, were all dressed up. They had combed their hair, were wear-ing shoes and stood in line to go to workshop to do piece work in order to earn their own benefits, their cigarettes and Coca Cola.

We did very simple things like that. I really loved those people, because when I grew up I knew what it was like to have everything and still to have nothing. Being raised as a triplet in a well-to-do household where I was loved, where I had all the material things, I still had absolutely nothing because nobody knew that I existed as an individual human being.

So instead of talking about the schizophrenic in room seventeen and the manic depressive in room fifty-three, I knew those people by name, I knew their idiosyncrasies, I knew their likes and dislikes. And they began to respond to me.

Two years later we were able to discharge ninety-four percent of these so-called hopeless, chronic schizophrenics, not on welfare but self-supporting in New York City. I was very proud of it.

I think that the greatest gift that those patients gave me was to teach me that there is something beyond drugs, beyond electroshock treatment, and beyond the science of medicine; that it is with real love and care that you can truly help people and make many, many people well.

What I'm trying to say to you is that knowledge helps, but knowledge *alone* is not going to help anybody. If you do not use your head and your heart and your soul, you are not going to help a single human being. In all my work with patients, I learned that whether they are chronic schizophrenics, severely retarded children, or dying patients, each one has a purpose. Each one cannot only learn and be helped by you, but can actually become your teacher. That is true of six-month old retarded babies who can't speak. That is also true of hopeless schizophrenic patients who behave like animals when you see them for the first time.

The Symbolic Language

The second gift my schizophrenic patients gave me was that I learned a language without which I would not have been able to work with dying children. That language is the symbolic, universal language that people all over the world use when they are in a crisis. If you are raised naturally — not normally because normally means terribly unnaturally — you would never have to read books on death and dying in order to work with dying patients, because you would be able to learn what needs to be done the way I learned it in Manhattan State Hospital. I always say — half joking, because I am serious about it — that the only honest people left on this earth are psychotics, young children and dying patients. And if you use these three kinds of people — and I mean "use" in a positive sense — if you can learn to hear, really hear them, they will teach you what we call the symbolic language.

People in pain, people in shock, people in numbness, people who are overwhelmed with a tragedy that they believe is beyond their comprehension, beyond their ability to cope with, use this language. Dying children, who are faced with their imminent death know it even if they have never been taught it. The symbolic language is a universal language, and it is used by all people all over the world.

There is no one dying, whether he is five or ninety-five, who does not know that he is dying. And the question is not: do I tell him that he is dying? The question is: can I hear him?

The patient may tell you for example, "I'll not be around for your birthday in July." It is good if you can hear that without your own need making you say, "Oh, don't talk like that. You are going to get well," because that would interrupt the communication between the patient and you, because the patient would understand that you are not ready to hear, and so you literally shut her up and she will feel very lonely.

But if you have no issues about death and dying, if you can acknowledge that this woman knows internally that she is close to death, then you sit with her and touch her, and you say, "Is there anything I can do for you, Grandma?" or whatever.

I was told of a young woman who was visiting her old grandmother. The old woman took the ring off her finger and gave it to her young granddaughter without saying a word. That is nonverbal, symbolic language. She simply put it on her granddaughter's finger. And this granddaughter didn't say, "Oh, Grandma, don't do that. You love this ring. I want you to keep it." Instead she said, "You really want *me* to have it?" And Grandma made like this: *(Elisabeth demonstrates how Grandma is nodding).* And then the granddaughter said, "Why don't you ..." and then she stopped what she intended to say which was, "Why don't you wait and give it to me for Christmas," because she immediately knew that Grandma must know that she would not be here at Christmas any more. And Grandma was very, very happy that she had the privilege to give the ring to her. She died two days before Christmas. That is symbolic, nonverbal language.

But very often the patients do *not* talk to you in plain English or plain Swedish. Many people feel your anxiety when you visit them. That makes them start talking about the weather. Not because they are interested in the weather, of course, but because they sense your anxiety and therefore keep their problems to themselves. The reason for this is that they don't want to add to *your* anxiety, because they are afraid that if they do, then maybe you will walk out on them and won't visit them any more.

When people try to convey to you their own awareness of a terminal illness, or any other tragedy for that matter, they will basically use three languages: one of them in Sweden would be plain Swedish. If the patients tell you when you are visiting them, "I know I have cancer. I am not getting out of this hospital any more," those are the people that you hear, those are the people that you help, those are the people that you respond to because they make it easy for you. They initiate your communication, they call a baby by its name. Those are the people that do *not* need your help. Because those terminally ill patients who can talk in plain Swedish or English about their own cancer and their own dying are the people who have already transcended their biggest fear, the fear of death. Actually they end up helping *you* and not the other way around. You may never admit it, but they are really *your* therapists, they are a gift to *you*. Those are not the people I am talking about tonight.

The people who need your help, who need it desperately, are the ones who are in a state of shock and numbness, people who are not prepared for the windstorms of life, people who have been pampered in life and for whom everything has been easy and smooth, people who come from families where they were protected from all hardships. Those people have been raised in a greenhouse. Sooner or later the windstorms hit them, and they are not prepared for them, like the parents who lost all their children to different forms of cancer within six months and were left childless. They were in such pain, such disbelief that this could happen to them, that they could not talk about it in plain English. And so they turned to the symbolic language instead. I beg you to learn this language so that you will be able to hear them.

There are two kinds of symbolic language: the symbolic nonverbal and the symbolic verbal language. Both are universal languages that you can use all over the world. And once you understand this language, which is the language that children use almost exclusively, then you will never have to guess, you will never have to gamble, and you will begin to understand that every single dying child, every single dying adult knows — not always consciously but subconsciously — that they are dying. They will share with you the one thing they need to share, and that is their unfinished business.

Some of you may know what a "parable" is. Jesus was very smart. He knew that He wanted to teach a lot of people what He came to teach. But the population wasn't ready; at least lots of them were not ready. And so He used parables, knowing that those who were ready to hear would hear. And the others are still scratching their heads two thousand years later. *(amusement from audience)* That is exactly the language that my dying children use when they pick *you* — and they do pick with whom they try that language. It may be a nurse's aide or somebody whom they think will be able to understand. Three-, four-year-old children look at you and they look through you and they know whether you can take it or whether you immediately will say, "Oh, children don't know about such things. He is just talking."

They use a language very similar to parables, a symbolic language, and if you nod when you don't know what they are talking about, you are very quickly written off as a phony-baloney. If you on the other hand understand that they are trying to tell you something but you have limited experience, then you might say, "You are trying to tell me something, but I'm not sure what it is. Say it again!" Then they will rephrase it in two, three, four or ten different variations until you do understand.

Most of the time it takes no more than one house call to help families and patients to evaluate — in a way to diagnose — their unfinished business and to help them get rid of it so they can move on and face their imminent death with peace and serenity and absence of fear and pain.

When a patient uses the symbolic language, it means that he is testing you out to see if you are ready for whatever he needs you for. Young children use almost exclusively the symbolic, nonverbal language. And the simplest, most beautiful, most helpful language that children use are drawings.

Susan Bach, a Jungian analyst from London, developed a method of looking at children's spontaneous drawings, children in Zurich at the hospital where I worked for fifteen years. She asked the children, who all had brain tumors, to draw a spontaneous picture, and then she discovered that they all revealed in their drawings their awareness of their pathology and even the location of the brain tumor.

And when she learned to analyze the drawings, she began to realize that the children not only were aware of what was happening inside their bodies but they also very often revealed how and when they were going to die.

When we have children who have leukemia, cancer or other illnesses, we ask them to draw a picture, and so they reveal their own inner sub-conscious awareness of their illness. Using the symbolic nonverbal language, we help them to finish their unfinished business and then they can help their own Mommies and Daddies to come to grips with their impending death.

Some of you have seen my book *To Live Until We Say Goodbye* and have seen the picture that five-year-old Jamie drew of a purple balloon floating up into the sky. Purple is the color of spirituality. Her concept of death was that in the very immediate future she would be a spirit floating up into the sky.

Children Losing a Relative

(Question from audience, "I would like to hear about children and their reactions after having lost a parent.") Children will react to the death of a parent depending on how they were raised before the death occurred. If parents have no fear of death, if they have not protected

their children but shared with them, for example, the death of a pet or the death of a Grandma, and if they have been allowed to participate in the care of their dying parent at home and also to go to the funeral, then you will have no problems with children.

This is one of the main reasons why we take young mothers and fathers home to die. The youngest child may be responsible for picking the favorite music of Mommy. Another child may be responsible for bringing tea. A third one may be responsible for something else. In this way the children *participate* in the care of the dying mother or father. When the time comes when the mother can no longer speak and when she goes into a coma during the last few days of her life, the children can still touch her, love her and hold her.

Then the children can be told that Mommy is in a coma like in a cocoon, that she is still very much alive and that she can hear everything they say. She can even listen to music. But she can no longer talk or respond. If the children are allowed to participate in this process, they will have an incredibly beautiful learning experience.

But if the mother is in a hospital or in an intensive care unit, especially in the United States where children are not allowed to come into the hospital, the children will have terrible nightmares about what they think that we are doing to their Mommy. And if on top of this they are not allowed to come to the funeral, then they will have a lot of fears and a lot of unfinished business, maybe for many years to come.

Our favorite motto is: *Should you shield the canyons from the windstorms, you would never see the beauty of their carvings.* That means that you should not shield your children, that you should not "protect" them, because you cannot protect them anyway. The only thing you will achieve is to protect yourself, while you prevent your children from getting an opportunity to grow and to prepare themselves for life.

Jamie's brother

Siblings have the biggest problem when you work with dying children, and the beautiful example that you can look at is in *To Live Until We Say Goodbye* where five-year-old Jamie, whom I mentioned before, died of a brain stem tumor. We were able to take her home. Her eight-year-old brother was allowed to participate in the care of his sister. He would come home from school, would very matter of factly say to his classmates that he had to go to work now, he would switch the oxygen on and very gently give her some oxygen. Then he would hop off the bed and when he would see that she needed some suctioning, with incredible love and tenderness, he suctioned her.

When she died he had no grief work whatsoever but only grief.

When the book came out with the photographs of him and his dying sister in it, I naturally went to show it to him, wondering how he would react to it. First he only looked at his own photographs, which is what all of us do, although we pretend that we look at the other pictures too *(laughter)*. When he had approved of his own photographs, he then looked at the whole chapter about his sister. His very beautiful response to it was, "I'm very glad that this came out in the form of a book. Because if my classmates lose a brother or a sister they can look at *my* book and know what they will have to do." He had a tremendous sense of pride and achievement and did not feel neglected and rejected like a great, great percentage of brothers and sister of dying children do.

When we have children whose mommy or daddy is dying, and the family asks "How in the world do we prepare the children?" you simply ask the children to draw a picture for you and then they go on to tell you how much they know about mommy's or daddy's immediate or imminent death. I will give you a practical example of this:

Lorrie

We had a school teacher who called us one day and described a first grader who had been doing wonderfully when school started, but started deteriorating rapidly a few months later. She couldn't understand why. She then called the child's home and was told by a very angry aunt that the child's mother was dying of cancer, had been in a hospital in a coma for two weeks, and was expected to die any day.

The teacher naturally asked the aunt if the children — the girl had a sister who was one year younger than her — were prepared for their mother's death. She said no. Not only had nobody told the children, but they had not seen their father for the last two weeks because, since the mother had gone into a coma, the young husband had been going to work earlier and earlier every morning to go straight to the hospital from work to be with his dying wife. By the time he came home, his two children were always asleep.

The teacher then very correctly said: 'somebody needs to talk to those children before it happens," and the aunt very angrily said, "Then *you* talk to them! But if you do it, do it now, because tomorrow it may be too late." Then she hung up on that poor teacher. Teachers have no preparation for this kind of work either.

The teacher phoned me and asked if I could help her. I told her that she could bring the children to my house after school under one condition, and that was that she stay with us in order to see what I was going to do with the children so the next time she would be able to do it herself. And she came.

I see all my dying patients in house calls, and any relatives have to come to my home for purely economical reasons. All the children who can walk, I see in my kitchen. I don't have a doctor's office because it is so scary for the children. I do not see them in the living room either. I see them in the kitchen because my kitchen has a fireplace and in Chicago, where it is sometimes 40 below zero, it is very nice to sit next to a fireplace.

I do something very 'horrible' and anti-holistic. I always serve Coca Cola and doughnuts *(laughter from audience)*. This is the unhealthiest food you can serve a child and I am aware of that as a physician. And I will tell you why I do that.

These are children who already have not been told the truth about their mother's condition. They already do not trust grown ups. They already are deteriorating in school. This means that they are very troubled and that they have no one to honestly communicate with. You can easily understand what would happen to such a distrustful kindergarten child or first grader if the teacher after school took them to a psychiatrist's private home and fed them with strange wheat germs or bean sprouts *(amusement in audience)*.

Instead we give them what they are most comfortable with. Whether this is healthy or not healthy is totally and completely and absolutely irrelevant at *this* time. It is very important that you hear that. Because we would be misusing our authority and our position if we tried to convert them at this time to healthier food habits. We grownups have a tendency to do that and the children turn us off, correctly so.

A year later maybe, when these children are my friends because we have helped each other through a very difficult time, they might be willing to hear me. Then I will invite them again to my kitchen and we can cook or bake some health foods together.

I have to say that because in the past when I didn't explain why I gave them Coke and doughnuts, I got incredibly hostile letters from people, and I don't need any more of those *(laughter from audience)*.

We usually sit down at the kitchen table with the children, and while they nibble on their doughnuts and drink their Coca Cola, I ask them to draw a picture. I give them a box of Crayola, and in two minutes I know that these children know. Then we can talk openly about it, and half an hour later they leave my house and they are OK, and it is *that* simple.

What this first grader drew was very beautiful. She drew a stick figure with enormous legs — bright red is always a color of danger — and next to it a kind of Indian design. Before finishing it, she crossed it out very angrily, again with red which is anger and pain.

I looked at the stick figure who had totally distorted legs and said, "I wonder if that is your mommy." She curtly said, "Yes."

I said, "My God, a mommy with legs like this must have trouble walking." She looked at me like she was testing me out, and she said, "My mommy's legs are so bad that she will never again walk with us in the park."

Then the teacher interfered — they always interfere *(amusement in audience)* — and said, "No, Dr. Ross, that is not true. Her mother is full of cancer. The only part of her body that is not affected by the cancer are her legs." And I said, "Thank you. But I don't want *your* reality. I need the child's reality." She understood what I meant.

Then I made a mistake. I went back to the child and said, "Lorrie, your mommy's legs must be horrible." And *very* annoyed she said,

"I *told* you that my mommy's legs are so bad that she will never again walk with us in the park." Like, "don't you hear?" *Then* I heard her.

Then I asked her about this funny Indian figure. She wouldn't tell me.

There are some tricks in this work that you will learn by trial and error. If you want a child to tell you the truth all you need to do is to guess wrong. Sooner or later they get tired of your stupid questions and tell you the truth *(laughter from audience)*.

But you cannot fake it. If I had known what this was and if I would have faked ignorance, the child would have looked through me instantly. But I really didn't know what that figure symbolized, so I guessed all sorts of things that were all wrong. And then, very annoyed, she said, "No, that's a tipped over table." I said, "A tipped over table?" And she said, "Yes, my mommy will never again have dinner with us at the kitchen table."

If a child tells you "never again" three times in three minutes, *you* will know that *she* knows. And so I switched from the symbolic language to plain English. I said to her, "Your mommy will never again eat dinner with you at the kitchen table and will never again walk with you in the park. To me that means that your mommy is not going to get well. To me that means that she's going to die." And she looked at me and said, "Yes!" implying, "What took you so long?" *(amusement in audience)*

And it is in that language... and that is how I mean it when I say, 'You do not tell *them*. They always, and I mean always, tell *you* — if you understand their language.'

I asked her what it meant to her that her mommy was going to die, and she said very quickly, "My mommy is going to Heaven." Then I said, "What does *that* mean to you?" And she closed her mouth very tight, took a step back and curtly said, "I don't know."

How many of you in this audience — if you try to behave like Americans for two minutes, and that means not to be shy *(amusement in audience)* — how many of you would say to two children like these with a dying mother something to the effect "Your mommy is going to Heaven"? *(silence in audience)*

Be a bit honest and put your hands up! *(coughing and uneasiness in audience)*

I see two hands. Would you believe that only two of you would do that? *(laughs and coughing)* Do you believe that?

If two kids with a mother who will die within two days asked you, "What is going to happen to my mommy when she dies?" How many of you in some way or other would say, "Your mommy will go to Heaven"? *(stirs in audience)*

Now we got about thirty hands! And if I kept on asking you another ten times I would slowly be coming close to the right answer *(laughs)*. I am trying to show this to you. And this is true everywhere in the world.

How many would never, ever, ever say, "Your mommy goes to Heaven"? *(A short silence. No hands. Amusement.)* That is the accurate number. Usually.

The reason why I am trying to show that to you is that most people, if they are honest and not afraid to say the wrong thing in public, would admit that. That is the most frequent statement that grown ups make to children. And that answer implies that your mommy is going to a good place where there is no more pain, no more suffering. That is really why you say it. But it *also* means, "Would you please shut up now! Don't ask any more questions and go out and play!" We don't admit that, but that is true.

What we grownups imply to those children is, "Your mommy goes to a good place where there is no more pain, no more suffering." And we hope that we convey that to those children. And the next day when mommy dies, the same grown ups cry and carry on like the greatest tragedy had happened. Do you understand why your children do not believe you?

This has been the biggest problem.

I told Lorrie, "I'm not going to talk about Heaven. I think that it's terribly important that you know what happens to your mommy right now. Your mommy is in a coma. A coma means that your mommy is like a cocoon. The cocoon looks like it's dead. Your mother cannot hug you any more. She cannot talk to you any more. She cannot respond to you any more. But she *hears* every single word you say. And very soon, in a day or two, what is going to happen to your mommy is what happens to a butterfly. When the time is right the cocoon opens up and the butterfly comes out." (That is the symbolic, verbal language.)

And we talked about butterflies and cocoons. She asked a lot of questions about mommy, and I asked the physician to break a rule — in American hospitals, children are not allowed to make visits. We called up and received permission from a very loving physician; he would smuggle those children into the hospital.

And I asked them if they wanted to see mommy once more to say all the things that they needed to say before mommy would die. The children very angrily said, "They won't let us," and I said, "Would you bet?" (That's how I win all my bets nowadays).

We believe very strongly that it is better to bring flowers to people during their lifetime than to pile them up on their casket. We believe very strongly that if people love music they should have music at a time like this. I asked the children for their mommy's favorite music. Their mommy loved John Denver. So we gave the children tapes with John Denver.

My consultation was over in about forty-five minutes. It was a lovely time spent, and it had incredible consequences. The teacher called up the next day and cried over the telephone and said that it was the most moving visit she had ever made to hospital.

She had opened the door to the hospital room, and there was this mother in a coma. Her husband was sitting *this* far away from the bed (*Elizabeth spreads her arms very wide*), a picture of total loneliness. Nobody touching.

The two little girls dashed into the room, jumped up on mommy's bed and with great joy and delight — they were not morbid and depressed and unhappy — they shared with mommy that they knew that she could not hug them any more, but that she could hear every word they said and that very soon, like in a day or two, she would be as free as a butterfly.

The father naturally started to sob and cry and finally hugged his children and communicated with them. The teacher, very appropriately, left them alone for some private, intimate sharing.

In the United States school system we have something called 'show and tell.' Children bring something special to school and are allowed to share that with the class.

The next morning Lorrie went to 'show and tell' in school. She went up to the blackboard, drew a cocoon and a butterfly coming out of the cocoon and shared with her class of first graders her visit to her dying mommy in the hospital, and thus gave what we considered the first Death and Dying Seminar to a class of first graders by a first grader. The only one who cried through the whole session was the school teacher.

The children began to open up and to share with Lorrie experiences of deaths in their own lives, usually the death of a pet, of a beloved animal, and sometimes of a grandma or a grandpa.

Because of this one shared moment with her mother, this child was able to reach the whole class of first graders.

But that's not all there is to it. What I try to share with you is that if you spend one hour with a child and share with her the experiences of death, it has the most incredible ramifications. Because without that hour I would not be here in Stockholm tonight.

In January, when I came back from Switzerland, I looked at my enormous pile of letters which, after Christmas with the Christmas cards, grows into the thousands and thousands. When I procrastinate, I always go to the kitchen and bake Christmas cookies for another day. I do that in May and August also *(amusement in audience)*. I looked at this enormous pile of unanswered mail and decided, "No. I just can't do that again." I decided to retire. I headed toward the kitchen and then I looked back at the pile once more and saw this big, yellow Manila envelope with the kind of big printed letters that little children write. I opened it up and I have baked no more Christmas cookies that year!

It was a gift from Lorrie. Her letter said, "Dear Dr. Ross, I would like to give you a consultation fee." She described how she was thinking about what she would give me, what would be meaningful, and she decided that she was going to give me the most precious gift that any child could ever, ever, ever give me. She gave me the whole collection of all the condolence letters that she had received from her classmates the next day when her mommy died. Every single letter was a drawing by a first grader with two or three lines written on it.

One letter said, "Dear Lorrie, I am very sad that your mommy died, but I guess it is only the shedding of a physical body, and maybe it was simply time to shed. Love, so and so." *(amusement in audience)*

What I am trying to convey to you is that if we grownups would be more honest, and instead of making such an incredible nightmare out of dying, we could convey to children where we are at and what we feel; if we would not be embarrassed to shed tears or to express our anger and rage (if we have any), and if we would not try to shield our children from the windstorms of life but instead share with them, then the children of the next generation will not have such a horrible problem about death and dying.

The Boy in San Diego

If you sit with a child and care for him, and if you are not afraid of his answers, then he will tell you practically everything about himself.

A few months ago I was in a bakery in San Diego to get some bread. I looked through the glass window and I saw a tiny little boy sitting on the curb. He looked *very* sad. I just had to go out and sit with him.

I sat there about half an hour without saying a word. I didn't move close to him, because I just knew in here *(indicating intuitive quadrant)* that if I came on too fast too soon, he would take off.

After about half an hour I said, short and matter of factly, something like, "It's tough." He said, "Uh huh."

After another fifteen minutes I said something like, "That bad?" He said, "Yes, I'm running away from home."

After another five minutes I said again, "*That* bad?" And without saying one single word he lifted his T-shirt up, and his whole chest

— I dropped my jaw — his whole chest was covered with burns from a hot iron. Front and back.

All this was symbolic, nonverbal language. I can sit for forty-five minutes you see, like a dog catcher, and I really care and sit with them and give them the space they need to share with me.

Interpretation of Children's Drawings

Older children write spontaneous poems, which is also the language of the soul, or they do collages to convey to you something that they cannot put into words. If you would be more honest — more like children — and if you don't understand what they try to convey to you, you say, "I don't understand. Explain it to me." Then they will explain it to you.

But if you just look at the collage and say, "Oh, that's nice!" and think that it is nothing, then you will miss the opportunity to understand what the child wanted to say to you. Some time ago they brought me my absolutely most incredible example of that, made by a fifteen year old girl.

It is my saddest but most practical example of symbolic, nonverbal language. I want all of you to see it. It's a collage. This fifteen year old girl asked everybody in the family to look at her collage, and she also asked the social worker. Nobody cared and took time enough to really look at it. And if any one of those people would had looked at it and understood the symbolic, nonverbal language, then this child would be alive today.

After having passed this collage around for two weeks, she committed suicide.

After she had committed suicide, the social worker sent me her collage saying, "Isn't that a wonderful example!"

Do you understand that this is very sad to me? It is so sad that this child had to die before the social worker learned to hear and listen to the girl's efforts to share her anguish and agony.

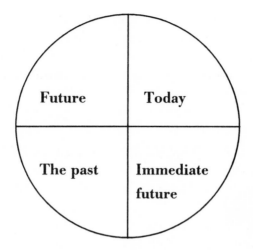

The four quadrants of a drawing according to Jung

I will point out some details in this collage for you.

It is very easy to read this collage. You don't have to be a psychiatrist, you don't have to "psychoanalyze" what you see. All you have to do is very simply to look at it, knowing a few basic things. Then you will understand how much all of us, and I mean everybody in here, how much all of us know inside. But up here *(indicating head)* you have only limited knowledge or awareness. If you want to get in touch with your inner knowledge which is far beyond anything you can put into words, try to get in touch with this and then you will also be able to hear your fellow man who really needs your help.

If you read this collage now you will understand that if somebody would have taken five or ten minutes time with this girl, she would probably still be alive.

According to Jung — I presume that all of you know who he was — you start looking at such a picture from the **left lower quadrant,** which is your past. And don't psychoanalyze it. Just read what it says. This girl made it easy for us. She made a combination of nonverbal, symbolic language and plain English. She even added words to it to be sure that somebody would be able understand it. Down below you read, "A suffering child needs your help." And you see a picture and what does the picture show? An ocean. What kind of an ocean? Is it a friendly inviting ocean? No, it's a dark scary ocean with no life boat and no lighthouse. There is nothing to hold on to. This is how she visually experienced her childhood. And that is scary and very, very lonely.

Then you go from there to the **right upper quadrant,** which is your today and which tells you how she felt at the moment she made this collage and what she is most afraid of today, the day she is making this collage. It says, "I'm crazy." She is afraid that she is going to be crazy. And the second biggest words are — you always start with the biggest pictures or the biggest writings and go to the smaller ones — the big question "Why?" And next to it, "Make friends with mommy." Which is the biggest image in the "now" quadrant? It's a mommy dog with puppy dogs. A family unit. The next picture is a baby clutching a doll to his chest. Then comes the smallest of the three pictures. It is a monkey who monkeys around. What do monkeys who monkey around stand for? It's like a clown who clowns to cover up his sadness. What does a monkey or a clown tell you about the prognosis? Anybody who can still monkey around has a chance because she still has a sense of humor. So she could still have been helped.

Now what is going to happen to her next week? The **right lower quadrant** is the immediate future. And what is going to happen in the immediate future to this fifteen year old girl? What are the words? "Fight to be free." And then, "Free again," and then, "Tough choice." And what is the image of her anticipated existence in a week from now? You see a forest where a big part of the forest has been chopped down already. In terms of prognosis: a glimpse of hope because there are new trees coming in the foreground. But what happens to the same monkey who a week earlier still monkeyed around? What is he doing now? He has stopped monkeying around. He is paralyzed. He is just sitting there numb, not playing anymore.

And then you go to the **left upper quadrant,** which is your concept of death and what you anticipate the future to hold. And that tells you how internally, from her spiritual, intuitive quadrant, she anticipates the outcome of her present situation. And what do you see? What does she know already? It is a hospital. And what happens in a hospital? A baby is born. What kind of a delivery? It's a baby that the doctor holds upside down. When do you hold babies upside down? When they don't scream, when they don't breathe. She already knew when she made this collage that she would be found not breathing and her hope was that she would get into the hands of a competent doctor who would bring her back to breathing. That is how you read those collages.

If that is not happening, what is the next biggest picture? A cat. What do cats stand for? Nine lives. If a doctor cannot bring you back to life, maybe there is something to what some people believe — that we have more lives than one. And if that is not possible, what is her last hope? I mean this collage tells you everything! What is the last picture? It's a lighthouse. You see down here in the left lower quadrant there is an ocean with no lighthouse. Up here it's a lighthouse of what some people experience: the light at the end of the tunnel. That is how you read those pictures.

⟁

You cannot get a more classical cry for help than this one, and it is even easy to see where the problem lies. But nobody saw it and that is the tragedy. When she was found, she had the collage with her, and, needless to say, the social worker felt very guilty for not having taken time out to look at it and to help her. And they sent it to me and asked me to promise that I would show it to all the grownups wherever they were listening to me. And if you forget the whole collage that's very OK, but do look at it and if another teenager who is suicidal or desperate gives you a collage, sit down and ask and he or she will be very glad that you cared enough to at least ask.

And that is essentially what we need to learn. To take time out for things that are essential. For being able to listen to our fellow man and for being able to hear what he has to say are essential. And also to learn the humility that if you don't understand what they are trying to tell us, then it is OK to say, "I don't know what you are saying. Can you rephrase it?" And once you open up the communication, you will find that it is not half as difficult as you thought that it would be.

Liz

Some time ago I was called to a twelve-year-old who was dying. We were able to take her home to die. I take all my children home to die if humanly possible. But we never put them in the bedroom because bedrooms are often used to punish children. I presume that it is not different here in Sweden. I think that you all remember that when you were naughty as a child you were sent to your bedroom and when you shaped up you were allowed to come out again. So many children associate the bedrooms with no-nos, taboos, punishment, and isolation.

Therefore, we take them into the living room in a big bed where they can see the forest, the garden, the clouds or the flowers, the birds, or the snow.

Liz was in a bed in the living room; very, very slowly dying of cancer. The mother was able to reach the girl in a very nice way. But the father was unable to say anything — he was an introvert and was incapable of talking about anything at all. But he was able to *show* her his love. He used to buy and bring home red roses, which he put on her table without a word. The whole family were very orthodox Catholics.

The father insisted that the other children (six, ten and eleven years old) did not know that their sister was dying. I did not believe that. I finally received permission from the father to see those children alone after school and have them draw a picture.

They drew pictures and it was very clear that they knew. Again, it was the six-year-old who started to switch from symbolic language to plain English. He said, "Yeah, she is going to die very soon." I said, "You know Peter, Liz is going to die in a day or two probably. If you have any unfinished business with her, do it now. Because you will feel much, much better if you don't postpone it until it is too late." Then he said, "Well, I am supposed to tell her I love her." I said, "No! You are not supposed to tell her 'I love you'. That is phony. You obviously have a lot of negative feelings inside, the way you sound."

And he finally blurted out, "Yeah. Sometimes I am terribly tired of her. I wish that she had dropped dead already." I said, "Yes, it has taken a long time. How come you're so impatient?" He said, "Well, I can't watch television, I can't slam the door, I can't bring friends home." Very natural things for a six year old. I was standing there helping him to say those things.

I told them that all children have the same feelings that he had, but only a few of them are brave enough to admit it. And now we were sitting here together and had the courage to say whatever we wanted to say. And you can be sure that they talked to their heart's content. It was fantastic.

I finally said to him, "I wonder if you're the only really honest person who can share that with your sister?" But he was already contaminated by the grown-ups so he said, "One ought not to say those things." I said, "You truly believe that if you feel and think those things, that your sister does not know it? How much more beautiful would it be if you could lovingly share that with her! And what a relief for her that somebody would really be open and loving with her."

I challenged him to it and he finally said that he would try.

We walk into this room. There is the bed. The six-year-old is next to his dying sister. I am behind him, ready to give him a little push if necessary. Behind me is the ten-year-old, then the eleven-year-old. From the door the mother appears, and behind the mother, the father. In chronological order of comfort! *(giggles from audience)*

The boy finally, after a little procrastination, blurted out: "sometimes I wished I could pray to get it over with." And the moment he said that the most beautiful consultation experience I had had in a long time happened. His twelve year old dying sister started to sob and sob and sob and cry. Not tears of pain, but of the greatest relief.

And she said, "Thank God, thank God, thank God, thank God, thank God!"

And then, when she recuperated from her tears, she finally explained why she felt this great relief. She said, "You know Peter, for the last three days and three nights already I have prayed to God to take me away. And every time I finish my prayer Mom comes in, stands at the door and tells me that she has been sitting up all night praying to God to keep me alive. But if you help me, Peter, we can outdo Mom." *(laughter from audience)*

Liz was so happy that they finally had stopped pretending, and they all hugged each other. And you understand that the six year old was the proudest young man in town, with the biggest, proudest grin on his face. And the beauty was that the mother heard her daughter saying that.

With this, the greatest problem was solved: both the parents and the children were prepared.

<hr>

But Liz could not die. For some reason she hung on to life. Three days later I went back. Medically speaking, it was incomprehensible that she was still hanging in there. I said to the mother, "she should have died at least a week ago. She is ready for it, she wants it, but she can't let go. I have tried everything. There is something that holds her back from letting go. I think that there is something that scares her. If it is OK with you, I am just going to ask her a straightforward question. But I want you to come with me, so you won't be worried over what I might have said to her. I want you to hear it yourself."

I said, "Liz, you can't die, can you?" And she said, "No."

I said, "How come?" She said, "Because I can't get to Heaven." Very surprised, I said, "Who told you that?"

The biggest problem with this kind of consultation is that, in trying to help one human being, you discover that you have to attack another one. It is very difficult to stop doing that, because you come across so much quackery, so much rubbish, so much scary nonsense that dying patients are told — in short, so much negativity, that it is very difficult not to become negative yourself.

Therefore I restrained myself when I asked her, "Who told you that?"

She told me that the priests and the nuns and the sisters who used to come to see her had told her many, many times that no one gets to Heaven unless she has loved God more than anybody else in the whole wide world. And then she leaned up again and with her skinny fingers that were ... her arms were like sticks of chalk and her belly looked like it was nine months pregnant. She tried to lean up at me and literally hang on to me and she whispered in my ear to prevent God from hearing her. She whispered in my ear, "You understand Dr. Ross, I love my mommy and daddy more than anybody else in the whole wide world." I was on the point of crying.

I find this incredibly sad. And the question is: how do you help a child like this? You *could* say nice words — and it would not help. You *could* say, "By loving mommy and daddy you also love God," or things to that effect — and it would not help. How do you help her to get rid of her feelings of guilt?

The only thing that works is for you to acknowledge *your own* negativity. We call it "the Hitler within us": when we get nasty, when we get critical, when we get judgmental, when we label people, when we don't like other people's methods.

And I was very angry at that priest who did that to Liz and at those nuns and sisters who use fear and guilt with little children.

But you understand, this is *my* problem, not Liz's problem.

So I told her, "I am not getting into an argument who is right and who is wrong. I'm only going to talk to you the way I always have."

That means I will now — for my own sake — go home and look at why I'm so critical, and put it temporarily into a drawer. But sooner or later I will have to deal with it so it does not interfere with my work. *Because you cannot do one positive thing to somebody in this world if you do it by knocking somebody else.*

I then used the symbolic verbal language. (It is the biggest gift to be able to use that language.) I said to her, "You and I have always talked about school. You were a very great honor student. The biggest dream in your life has always been to become a teacher. And the only time since I learned to know you that I ever saw you devastated was in September when the school year started and the school bus came and you looked through the window and you saw your friends and your brothers and sisters getting up on the school bus."

One month earlier she had been told that she was cured, but just before school started they had discovered the first metastases. I went on, "And I think for the first time in your life, it hit you that you would never, ever again be on that school bus, that you would never again be able to go to your beloved school, that you would never become a teacher."

And she said, "Yes."

I said, "I want you to answer me one single question. Sometimes it happens that your teacher gives *very* tough assignments. Does she give these super tough assignments to her worst students? What I would like to know is if she gives these assignments to the worst pupils in the class, or if she gives them to just anybody in the class. Or does she give them only to very few of her best, chosen students?"

Then her face lit up — I have never seen anything like it — and she said, "Oh, she gives them to *very* few of us." She was one of the best pupils in her class and was very proud of it. And I said: "since God is also a teacher, what do you think: did He give you a tough assignment, or did He give you one that He could have given to just any child in the class?"

Then again, in the symbolic, nonverbal language, she looked down at her poor, devastated body — her *very* huge belly and her very skinny arms and legs. She looked down at her body like she was evaluating the tests of her life. Then she smiled a happy smile and dead seriously she said, "I don't think God could give a tougher assignment to any child."

And I didn't have to add, "What do you *now* think that He thinks of you?"

The last nonverbal communication I had with Liz was a few days later when I went back, more to see how the other children were doing.

She was slipping into a semiconscious state. I stood under the doorway, taking a last look at her, really to say good-bye to her in a silent way. She suddenly opened her eyes, obviously recognized me, and again with this big, almost smirk, almost happy grin on her face, she looked down at her belly like, "I got your message."

This is how we try to help children to finish their unfinished business. It is very easy to work with dying patients. It is even more easy to work with dying children because they are less complicated. They are very straightforward. And the beauty, the incredible beauty about children is that when you make a boo-boo they give you instant feedback. If you make a mistake you know it immediately.

We will try to teach the symbolic language not only to medical students, but to seminary students, to teachers and to nurses, so that they can better learn to understand the language of the ones who are in most need of their help.

Those of you who have children: listen, really listen to your children and you will learn a language that is more important than Esperanto or English or Spanish or any world language because it is the language of the needy people. And the exchange that you get for learning it are gifts to help you to live fully.

When you listen to dying patients who have been able to finish their unfinished business, you will find that for the first time in their life they learn what it means to live fully.

Dougy

A few years ago I was giving a lecture in Virginia. You may not know this, but I hate lecturing. It is terrible to stand on the stage, you know, day after day, basically saying the same things. And in those days I used to lecture from nine A.M. to five P.M. So I needed some fuel. My fuel was to read the audience to see if there was somebody interesting there; you know, I guess who they are and what they are doing. It's . . . it's a game that I play.

That particular day I was looking around the audience saying to myself, "You will have to talk to this group all day." In the front row sat a couple. The moment I looked at them I had this incredible urge — which you understand does not come from the intellectual quadrant but from the intuitive, spiritual quadrant — to ask them why in the world they hadn't brought their child to my lecture.

Well, *(she laughs a little)* I would say that a normal psychiatrist doesn't do that. I don't think that exists *(laughter from audience)*. I mean, you don't say a thing like that from the stage while you are giving a lecture. I really had to control myself not to ask them. If I had, people naturally would have said that I was crazy. But on the other hand, other people's opinion of me is their problem, not mine. Right?

But I made a physiologic break very early — much too early — and I went to this couple. They were very down-to-earth, regular people. I phrased my question in a socially acceptable way, saying, "I don't know why I need to say this, but I have this urge to ask you: why didn't you bring your child here?"

And they didn't laugh at me. They just looked at me and said, "It's interesting that you should say that, because we debated early this morning if we should bring him, but the problem is that today is the day of his chemotherapy."

As you can see, their answer already confirmed to me: yes they have a child, it is a boy, he has cancer and he is on chemotherapy. I said, "I don't know why I am saying this, but it is very urgent that he be here."

They knew unconditional love, and the father left during the break. About eleven o'clock he came back with his adorable nine-year-old boy who was wide-eyed, very pale, and totally bald from the treatment. They all sat in the front row. The boy took in every word I said.

And the father gave him a box of Crayola and a piece of paper. To keep him quiet, *he* thought. To *me*, it was divine manipulation, not chance.

At the twelve o'clock lunch break — it was the usual chicken lunch, which I have five times a week so I skip it *(laughter from audience)* — he came up with his Crayola picture and said, "Dr. Ross, this is a present for you." I thanked him and looked at it and... I am a translator, to translate is my main job, so I looked at his picture and I said to him without thinking (this little guy wasn't there when I was talking about the drawings) I said to him, "Shall we tell 'em?"

He immediately knew what I was talking about. He looked at his parents and said, "Yes, I think so." I said, "Everything?" He looked at them again and said, "Yes, I think that they can take it."

Nine-year-old children who have a terminal illness are wise, old souls. All children are very old, wise souls if they have suffered, if their physical quadrant has deteriorated before adolescence. God created man in such a miraculous way that the spiritual quadrant, which usually does not emerge until adolescence, begins to emerge prematurely to compensate for the loss of the physical abilities. This is why young dying children are very old, wise souls if you understand that symbolically speaking. They are much wiser than children who are healthy and have been raised in a greenhouse. That is why we always tell parents, "Do not protect your children! Share your anguish and your pain with them. Otherwise they will develop into cripples. Because sooner or later the plants have to come out of the greenhouse anyway and then they cannot withstand the cold and the winds."

So I looked at his picture, and because I am in town only one night, usually I don't want to open up something or hurt somebody and then not be available the next day. So I always double-check. And I didn't trust the mother. She looked very vulnerable. So that is why I asked the boy, "Shall we tell them all of it?" Do you understand what we were talking about? "Shall I read your picture to your parents?"

He looked at them again and said, "Yeah, I think that they can take it." I still didn't trust the mother so I asked her, "What is your biggest, biggest fear?" She started to cry and said, "We were just told that he has three months to live."

I looked at Dougy's picture and said, "Three months? No. Impossible. Out of the question. Three years maybe. But three months is totally out of the question."

She hugged me and kissed me and thanked me. I said, "don't do that. I am a translator and a catalyst. It is your son who knows those things. I am only translating his inner knowledge. I am not responsible for giving you three years of your child's life."

We became very fast friends. During the afternoon lecturing I watched him like a hawk. About a quarter to five he started to get sleepy. I stopped my lecture because *I* wanted to say good-bye to him. The last thing I said to him was, "Dougy, I cannot make house calls in Virginia very often. But if you ever need me, the only thing you have to do is to write. And because I'm always a thousand letters behind, write the envelope yourself. You see, children's letters are always priority number one. And to be on the safe side write 'personal' on it." And I spelled it out to him.

I am at home only one day a week and most of the time I only have time to go through the children's letters. Grown-ups have misused that fact since. They have imitated children's writing by printing on the envelopes. If any grownups do that I refuse to answer because that is misusing my trust and that would in the end only feed into negativity.

Anyway, I waited and waited and no letter came, and you know how your head begins to interfere. I said, "Oh my God suppose he has died, I gave the parents false hope, and I . . ." I mean the whole head trip. And the longer your head trips are the more you become worried and negative. But one day I decided, "That's ridiculous. My intuition is *very* accurate and my head is very *not* accurate many times. So forget your worries!"

And the day after I let go of my worries I had a letter from him. It was the most beautiful letter I have ever received during my twenty years of working with dying patients. It was a two liner, "Dear dr. Ross, I have only one more question left. What is life and what is death and why do little children have to die? Love, Dougy."

Do you understand why I am prejudiced for children? They cut through all the baloney *(laughter)*. So I wrote him a letter and I couldn't write him, you know, big stuff. I had to write to him the way he wrote to me.

So I borrowed my daughter's gorgeous felt tip pens in twenty-eight colors, marvelous colors, and folded a paper up and then I folded another paper and it finally ended up in a little booklet all printed in rainbow colors, every letter a different color. It looked very pretty, but it still didn't look finished so I started to illustrate it. And then it was ready to be mailed off.

Then I had a problem. I liked it *(laughter from audience)*. And I really liked it so much that I wanted to keep it and my head immediately came to my rescue. You see, after death you know that the highest goal in life is to always take your highest choice. To keep the letter for myself wouldn't have been my highest choice but my head came to my rescue and said, "You are entitled to keep it. You can use it for your house calls with dying children. It will help the brothers and sisters of the dying child." And the longer the excuses became, the more I knew that I'd better go to the post office fast.

So I finally said to myself, "No. I'm not going to wait twenty-four hours in order to copy it. I'm gonna send it off right now, because if he dies now and the letter arrives too late, I will feel very bad. And I really made it for him, not for me."

I let go of it and mailed it.

The rewards always come back a thousand times if you take the highest choice. Because a few months later — it was last March — he called up long distance from Virginia to California and said, "I wanted to give you a birthday gift for my birthday." And he told me that he had showed it to so many parents of dying children, and all of them wanted a copy, and therefore he decided that he would give me permission to print it, so that I could make it available to other children.

We have printed it and we call it *The Dougy Letter.*

Now I'll show you how horrible it is when you are not honest. Even with good motivations you will always get into trouble sooner or later. Some months ago I was called to a very, very famous talk show in New York City, where you talk for three minutes to ten million people and can't even say one important thing, because you have such a short time. They ask you one question and you answer it and then you are off the air. I have always wondered why people do that. But I did it too.

And instead of asking me what I wanted to say in three minutes that would be meaningful, they asked me about the five year old Jamie, who is in my book *To Live Until We Say Goodbye.* The next day I got a very angry letter from Dougy. He wrote, "I don't understand you. Why did you have to talk about Jamie? Why couldn't you talk about me? Because if all those people had bought one *Dougy Letter* I would have been able to see my daddy again."

His daddy has, like most Americans, $200,000 debts for doctor and hospital bills. And in order to pay those bills he moonlights and has double jobs and has a weekend job as well. He very seldom has time to see his boy.

I don't think that here in Sweden you are aware of the kind of problems associated with terminal illnesses. You see, the big mistake I made was that when the family didn't have enough money to eat, I sent them a check. And in order not to make it look like a welfare check I made the mistake to write on the check, "For royalties." I made them believe that this was from the sales of *Dougy*

Letters. And now this poor child expects to get such a check every six months. And I am in real trouble *(laughter from audience).*

So every patient you work with is teaching you something, and it is not always that it has to do with death and dying, but with life and living.

The Meaning of Suffering

Dying patients, when you take your time and sit with them, teach you about the stages of dying. When you know that you are going to die soon, you go through the denial and the anger, and the "Why me?" and you question God and reject Him for a while. You bargain with Him, and you go through horrible depressions.

What does hope mean for you when you are dying? When you are told that you have a terminal illness, first you always think, "Oh, it is not true, it must be a mistake." Then you hope that it's operable or curable. If that's not true, you then hope that chemo-therapy or visualization or whatever at least will take care of your symptoms and that you will be functioning and relatively healthy. Then you acknowledge that no matter how much you take in an experimental drug, you just get worse, and then you get well again and worse again. It goes up and down. Is there a point when you give up? No! There isn't a point where you give up. Whatever happens to you in terms of ups and downs, every experience that every human being in the world has is for a purpose. It will teach you one specific thing that you would otherwise not learn. And God doesn't give you any more tests than you need.

When you have passed a test you may do quite well for a while, and then something new will happen. You become blind, or your diarrhea starts again, or this or that starts again. All of us find out, you know, what is behind all this. And you fight again if you are a fighter, and if you are somebody who resigns very quickly, then you resign very quickly, but the trouble is not going to go away. So if you can find behind the trouble what you can learn...

And if you have another human being who cares, you may be able to reach a stage of acceptance.

But that is not just typical of dying; really it has nothing to do with dying. We only call it the "stages of dying" for lack of a better word. If you lose a boyfriend or a girlfriend or if you lose your job, or if you are moved from your home where you have lived for fifty years and you have to go to a nursing home, and even if you only lose a parakeet or your contact lenses, you may go through the same stages of dying.

This is, I think, the meaning of suffering: all the hardships that you face in life, all the tests and tribulations, all the nightmares and all the losses, are still viewed as curses by most people, as punishments by God, as something negative. If you would only know that nothing that comes to you is negative! I mean nothing. All the trials and tribulations and the biggest losses that you ever experience, things that make you say, "If I had known about this, I would never have been able to make it through," are gifts to you. It is like somebody who has to...*(turns to audience)* What do you call it when you make the hot iron into a tool? You have to temper the iron.

Every hardship is an opportunity that you are given, an opportunity to grow. To grow is the sole purpose of existence on this planet Earth. You will not grow if you sit in a beautiful flower garden and somebody brings you gorgeous food on a silver platter. But you will grow if you are sick, if you are in pain, if you experience losses and still don't put your head in the sand, but take the pain and learn to accept it, not as a curse or a punishment, but as a gift to you with a very, very specific purpose.

I will now give you a clinical example of that. In one of my one-week workshops — they are one-week live-in retreats — there was a young woman. She did not have to face the death of a child, but she faced several what we call "little deaths," although not very little in her own eyes. When she gave birth to a second baby girl, which she was very much looking forward to, she was told in a not very humane way that the child was severely retarded. In fact the child would never even be able to recognize her as a mother. When she became aware of this, her husband walked out on her. Suddenly she was faced with a very difficult situation. She had two young, very needy, very dependent children, and she had no money, no income and no help.

She went through a terrible denial. She couldn't even use the word "retardation."

After that she went through a fantastic anger at God and cursed him out. First He didn't exist at all. Then He was a mean old... you know what. After that she went through a tremendous bargaining — if the child at least would be educable, or at least could recognize her as a mother. Then she found some genuine meaning in having this child, and I will simply share with you how she finally resolved her problem. It began to dawn on her that nothing in life is a coincidence. She tried to look at this child and tried to figure out what purpose a little vegetable-like human being could have on this Earth. Finally she found the solution, and I am sharing this with you in the form of a poem that she wrote. She is not a poet, but still it is very moving. In the poem she identifies with her child who talks to her godmother. She calls the poem "To My Godmother."

To My Godmother

What is a godmother?
I know you're very special.
You waited many months for my arrival.
You were there and saw me when only minutes old,
and changed my diapers when I had been there just a few days.
You had dreams of your first godchild.
She would be precocious like your sister,
You'd see her off to school, college, and marriage.
How would I turn out? A credit to those who have me?
God had other plans for me. I'm just me.
No one ever used the word precocious about me.
Something hasn't hooked up right in my mind.
I'll be a child of God for all time.
I'm happy. I love everyone, and they love me.
There aren't many words I can say,
But I can communicate and understand affection, warmth,
    softness and love.
There are special people in my life.
    Sometimes I sit and smile and sometimes cry.
    I wonder why?
    I am happy and loved by special friends.
    What more could I ask for?

Oh sure, I'll never go to college, or marry.
But don't be sad. God made me very special.
I cannot hurt. Only love.
And maybe God needs some children who simply love.
Do you remember when I was baptized,
You held me, hoping I wouldn't cry and you wouldn't drop
    me?
Neither happened and it was a very happy day.
Is that why you are my godmother?
I know you are soft and warm, give me love,
    but there is something very special in your eyes.
I see that look and feel that love from others.
I must be special to have so many mothers.
No, I will never be a success in the eyes of the world,
But I promise you something very few people can.
Since all I know is love, goodness and innocence,
Eternity will be ours to share, my godmother.

This is the same mother who, a few months before, was willing to let her toddler crawl out near the swimming pool while pretending to go to the kitchen so the child would fall into the swimming pool and drown. A tremendous change has taken place in this mother.

This is what takes place in all of you if you are willing always to look at what happens in your life from both sides. There is never just one side to it. You may be terminally ill, you may have a lot of pain, you may not find somebody to talk to about it. You may feel that it is unfair to take you away in the middle of your life, that you have not really started to live yet. Then look at the other side of the coin and you are suddenly one of the few fortunate people who are able to throw overboard all the baloney that you have carried with you in your life.

When you have done that, you will be able to go to somebody and say, "I love you" when he can still hear it, and after that you can skip the schmaltzy eulogies. And as you know that you are here for a very short time, you can finally do the things that you really want to do. How many of you in this room do exactly what you love to do? I mean *totally* live? *(a very few hands)* How many do not? *(more hands)* Would you change your work on Monday? *(laughter)*

It is very important that you only do what you love to do. You may be poor, you may go hungry, you may lose your car, you may have to move into a shabby place to live, but you will *totally* live. And at the end of your days you will bless your life because you have done what you came here to do. Otherwise, you will live as a prostitute, you will do things only for a reason, to please other people, and you will never have lived. And you will not have a pleasant death.

If on the other hand you listen to your own inner voice, to your own inner wisdom, which is far greater than anybody else's as far as you are concerned, you will not go wrong and you will know what to do with your life. Then time is no longer relevant.

The hardest lesson that people have to learn is to learn unconditional love. And that is very hard to learn. Virginia Satir, whom some of you may know, described very beautifully what unconditional love is all about. She says:

> I want to love you without clutching,
> appreciate you without judging,
> join you without invading,
> invite you without demanding,
> leave you without guilt,
> evaluate you without blaming
> and help you without insulting.
> If I can have the same from you,
> then we can truly meet and enrich each other.

Elisabeth Kübler-Ross on Kodiak Island, Alaska (seeing eskimo patients)

Elisabeth Kübler-Ross in Japan (1993)

The Cocoon & the Butterfly

The first time I was here in Sweden was 1947. A lot of things have changed since then. If anybody would have told me in 1947 what I'd be doing today, I don't know whether I would have had the courage to get started.

Two days ago I was in Duisburg, and the first thing that greeted me was those people with the big signs about bomb threats and bomb detection machines. I wondered why people feel so threatened by somebody who works with dying children.

I will talk very briefly as a psychiatrist to help you understand the main lessons that we have learned from working with dying patients. Dying patients not only teach us about the process of dying but also what we can learn about how to live in such a way that we have no unfinished business.

People who have lived fully will neither be afraid of living nor of dying. And to live fully means that you have no unfinished business, and that in turn means that you have to be raised in a way very few of us and our children have been raised. I am sure that if we had one generation of children that were raised in a natural way, the way we were created, we would not need to write books on death and dying and have seminars and have these horrendous problems with one million children disappearing and thousands of them dying prematurely by suicide and homicide.

The Four Quadrants

Every human being consists of four quadrants: a physical, an emotional, an intellectual and a spiritual/intuitive quadrant.

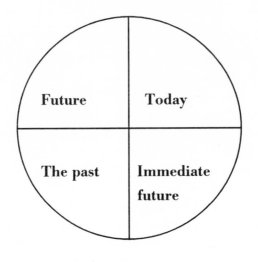

The Four Quadrants

When we are born, we are exclusively **physical** human beings, and during the first year of life, in order to grow up in a natural way, neither afraid of living nor of dying, we need a lot of loving, hugging, touching and physical contact. Then at the end of our life, when we are old Grandmas or Grandpas living in nursing homes, then again the one aspect of our life that we are missing the most is that we are not touched, loved and hugged enough. In our society the only people usually who give us totally unconditional love were the very old people: our Grandmas and Grandpas.

In a society where every generation lives all by themselves — the old people in nursing homes, sick people in hospitals, children at school — most children miss that aspect of growing up. And that gives the children their first problems in the development of their **emotional** quadrant (between the ages of one and six) where they get all their basic attitudes that will mark them for life.

Our children need to be raised with unconditional love and firm consistent discipline, but with no punishment. That sounds easy, but it is not easy. But it *is* possible to dislike their behavior and still love them. If you are able to do that, the children develop a very beautiful **intellectual** quadrant at around the age of six; they love to learn, and going to school is a challenge, not a threat.

My big dream before I die is to start E.T.-centers. And that is to change old age homes into E.T.-centers. Is there anybody here who has not seen the movie, "E.T."?

E.T.-centers are homes for the Elderly and Toddlers. You skip one generation. You will have no problems. The old people who have contributed to society for seven decades are entitled to have a home of their own — a nice, private place with their own furniture — and they would live on the first floor. And the only payment they would have to make would be to take care of one child and spoil that child rotten. They would have to pick a child who appeals to them the most from among the toddlers of working parents. The parents will bring them in in the morning when they go to work and pick them up at the end of the day.

The gift that they give to each other would be of mutual benefit. The old people would be touched again. Little children love wrinkled faces. They even like pimples. They play piano on them (*laughter from audience*). And old people need more hugs and touches and kisses — especially from children. The children in the first few years of their lives would learn total, unconditional love. If you have lived with unconditional love early in life, things can get very bad later on in life, and you will still be able to cope with it. If you have experienced unconditional love once, it will last for your whole lifetime. It does not have to be from your father or your mother, who may not be capable of giving it, because they themselves have never received it. That is my E.T.-center dream.

In adolescence you would very naturally develop your **spiritual, intuitive** quadrant. This is how we would develop normally and naturally, if we were permitted a natural evolution through growing up with no interference. The spiritual, intuitive quadrant is that part of you that has all knowledge. It is the only quadrant in the human being that we do not need to work for, because we are born with it. We are also given a gift: if we lose something we always get something in return that is better than the part we lost. In children who die at a young age of leukemia, brain stem tumor, or what have you, the physical quadrant deteriorates. The gift that they receive in its place — and we grownups do not appreciate this

enough — is that their spiritual quadrant begins to emerge, sometimes already at the age of three, four or five. The longer they have
suffered and the more they have suffered, the sooner this evolves.
They will look like tiny children — much younger than their chronological age — but their spiritual quadrant is so wide open that they
talk like old, wise people.

These children come to this earth to be our teachers. If we do not
hear them, if we pretend that they are too young to know about
dying, or if we play games with them, then *w e* are the losers, not the
children.

The problem is that very few of us are totally intuitive, that most
of us do not listen to ourselves, but listen to others to tell us what to
do. And that is because most of us were raised with conditional
love. If you have been raised with, "I love you if you bring good
grades home," "I love you if you make it through high school,"
"God, would I love you if I could say: my son the doctor," then you
have been raised with the belief that you can buy love, that your
parents will love you if you become what your parents want you to
become. And you end up becoming a prostitute *(scattered laughs fro m
audience)*. Prostitution is the biggest problem in this world because
of this one word, "if." There are millions of people who would do
anything, anything in the world, to make sure that their parents
love them. Anything. Those are the people who believe that you
can buy love. They shop around until the end of their lives, shop-
ping for love, and they never find it. Because you cannot buy real
love. And they are the ones I see on their death bed saying very
sadly to me, "I have made a good living, but I have never really
lived." Then you ask them, "What does it mean to you to really
live?" And they say, "Well, I was a very successful lawyer, or a very
successful doctor, but I really wanted to be a carpenter."

When you work with dying patients, first you exclusively take
care of their physical needs, their physical quadrant. You will have
to keep your patients first and foremost pain free. Physical comfort
and absence of pain comes long before any emotional support, be-

fore any spiritual help, before anything else. You cannot help a dying patient emotionally or spiritually if he is climbing up the wall with pain, or if you on the other hand give him pain injections that make him so dopey and sedated that he cannot communicate any longer.

And so what we do is to give the patients an oral pain cocktail that is given before they have any pain, and that is given to them regularly, so that they always are pain free and conscious until the moment they die. All this is a pre-requirement for emotional support.

When they are comfortable physically, pain free, not left alone, dry and able to communicate, then you move on to the emotional quadrant.

But how do you communicate with a terminally ill patient who cannot say a word? How do you communicate with a patient who has ALS or has had a massive stroke and is totally paralyzed up to here? How do you ever figure out that he, for example, wants you to scratch his back? You are not mind readers — very few people are — so how do you communicate with him? Well, you make a speaking board: you make a list of the alphabet, a list of all the important persons, a list of all the body parts, then a list of all the important physiological needs. Then even a ten year old child can go up and down on these lists and the patient can go "Hrrr" when he points at the right word or the right letter.

This speaking board is a God-given gift for ALS patients. It has not all that worth for stroke patients because many of them cannot comprehend written words. So for stroke patients, you will have to make a board of pictures instead.

It is important that you know about the speaking board, because if a patient is totally intelligent and lies on his back for four years and cannot communicate with you in any way, then you will begin to treat him like he is deaf and dumb because there is no response coming from him. And people disconnecting from you is one of the worst deaths you can experience.

I had a consultation a few years ago requested by the wife of a middle aged man who had been paralyzed and unable to speak for four years.

When I saw the patient, he was a very devastated man lying flat on his back. He had two small children and a *very* exhausted wife. And all he could express was total panic.

I used a speaking board and asked him why he was in such a panic and he answered that his wife was trying to get rid of him. I said, "She is trying to get rid of you? But she has been taking care of you for four years day and night, twenty-four hours a day!" He said, "Yes. That's why she is trying to get rid of me. She has had it. She cannot take any more and she has made arrangements to send me to a hospital." Now he was afraid that in the last few weeks of his life, she would send him off to a hospital, and he knew hospitals well enough to know that they would put him on a respirator.

He said that for four years he had been watching his children grow up, and that he was able to cope with his disease. And now in the last few weeks of his life, he said, his wife couldn't take it any more and wanted him to go to the hospital. He begged her to please hang in there another couple of weeks, and he promised her to die soon, so that it would not be such a burden on her.

I asked her right in front of the patient and the children if he was right, and she confirmed that she had made arrangements to make the hospital take him because she was at the end of her physical strength. All of you who have ever taken care of a patient twenty-four hours a day know that no human being can do that for four years. And I asked her what it would take to hang in there another few weeks. Because if a patient who is *not* neurotic tells you that he has only a couple of weeks to live, then you should listen to him!

And she said, to make a long story short, that she needed a man. And I asked her if it was that difficult to live without a man. And she said no, she had gotten used to not having a husband, but the reason she needed a man was that she needed a strong person who could take over the night shift from 8 P.M. to 8 A.M., so she could sleep through a whole night. I think that any one of you who have had a sick child knows that this is a very reasonable request.

I believe that there are no coincidences in life — I call them "divine manipulations." I knew that I made this house call the night before a five-day workshop and I said, "You know, I'm sure I'm here because in this workshop will be *just* the right man. And I will kidnap him and bring him here *(amusement from audience)* to take over your night shifts. And just in case this does not happen, I will come back and make another house call."

And this woman had so much faith in what I call divine manipulation that she said she would hang in there for another five days.

Then the workshop started. We always have more women than men, naturally. I only looked at the men *(amusement from the audience)*. I looked at every man in this group of one hundred people. I said to myself, "Maybe that's the man? No. Maybe him? No." Nobody looked right.

And by Wednesday I started to get nervous *(amusement from audience)*. Usually my intuition is very good. It's when I use my head that I get into trouble *(amusement from audience)*. But by Wednesday I looked at every man except the one who had not yet shared.

And then this man came up and he started to share, and at the *moment* he opened his mouth I said, "*No way* is he going to take care of this patient." He talked, if you excuse the expression, like a Californian *(laughter from audience)*. That's a nasty expression, I don't mean it nasty. He was sitting like... folded up *(tries to demonstrate how he was sitting)*. I can't sit that way.

He shared how he went from workshop to workshop from Esalen to the Himalayas. He lived on brown rice and raw vegetables *(amusement from audience)*. I cannot describe him more grotesquely, but he was one of these *real* extremists *(amusement from audience)* who had workshopitis *(laughter from audience)* and I regard these people as parasites because they never work, they just go from workshop to workshop *(laughter)* And the more he talked the more I said, "No, no, no. I can't send such a person to this man."

And at the end of his sharing he said, "I want to go in your footsteps. I want to do this kind of work." And I thought, "I'm gonna show you." *(amusement from audience)* I said, "Are you willing to work twelve hours a day?"

"YES!"

"Are you willing to work with a man who can't speak?"

"Yes!"

"Who can't write notes?"

"Yes!"

"Day and night?"

"Yes!"

"Are you willing not to get paid for your work?"

"Yes!"

The worse I described the patient the more excited he got *(amusement from audience)*. And at the end I had no way out but to tell him, "OK. Your work starts at Friday night 8 P.M." *(laughter from audience)*

I must say that I had absolutely no expectations that he would show up at work. I thought, "When the workshop is over at noon Friday, he will disappear."

But he not only started to work for this family, he did the best job anybody has ever done for any of my patients. From foot massage to cooking special meals, to reading to the patient. He was *really* taking care of him. And he stayed until two weeks after his death to be sure that the family was OK.

And the lesson *I* learned is never to underestimate a Californian *(big laughter form audience)*. You never, ever, ever . . . Any time you react negatively to a person or to anything you must understand that this is your own unfinished business. Do you hear that? I reacted much longer than fifteen seconds to that man, so I had to go home and look at what turns me off when I hear about brown rice and raw vegetables *(laughter from audience)*. That's because I drink coffee and eat hamburgers and smoke cigarettes and I am very allergic to this extremist health food stuff *(amusement from audience)*. But that's the way you diagnose your own unfinished business. And it is very important that you do that.

❦

So after you take care of the physical needs of your patient, after you have been sure that there is a way to communicate — and there is never no way to communicate if you know about the speaking board — then only is it possible to take care of the emotional quadrant.

All you need to do as a helper is to ask what you can do for them and hear and listen to the dying patients who tell you, from their intuitive quadrant, not from their intellectual quadrant, what it is that they need to do in order to live, literally to live, until they die.

But you have to be aware of the fact that many, many patients share with you that they *don't* want your help. They tell you in a polite and sometimes in a not very polite way that you should go home, what are you doing here?

Most people who offer their help feel terribly rejected when they are told to go home. But you have to appreciate that if you were dying and you were in a hospital and somebody came and offered to help you finish your unfinished business you would say, "No thank you!" because you would like to choose your own friend with whom to finish unfinished business and you would not like a hospital administrator to send someone in to do it for you.

We should always evaluate when a patient makes us feel unloved, unwanted or unneeded, because every time you get negative about anybody, especially a patient, he gives you a gift by getting you in touch with your own unfinished business. If you have enough self-worth and self-respect and a feeling of confidence about the role that you play, you will not be devastated when a patient tells you, "No, thank you!" It is very important that people in the health professions learn that, in order not to become "burned out." *You may work eighty hours a week with dying children, with the families of murder victims and suicide and with the greatest tragedies that you can barely conceive, without ever, ever getting burned out as long as you have no unfinished business yourself.*

The Five Natural Emotions

God created man with five natural emotions. They are fear, guilt, anger, jealousy and love. And by the time you are six all the natural emotions have been turned into unnatural ones. Anything on the natural side will maintain your energy and anything on the unnatural side will strain you to such a point that you will call it a burn-out syndrome. How many of you have experienced a burn out? *(several hands)* It does not exist! *(surprised laughter from audience)* A burn-out is as ridiculous as saying, "The Devil made me do it." *(laughter from audience)* The Devil doesn't make you do anything if you don't let him. The burn-out is . . . say that you work in the ICU and you have five patients dying in one day. Then there is the sixth one coming in and it's an hour before you are allowed to leave and you are going to be stuck with that patient and you say, "I can't take another one." And you never share your frustration, your impotence, your rage, your anger, your feelings of unfairness. You are the care giver and you keep a lid on all your frustrations and your negativity because you can't go round sobbing and crying or beating the doctors up. And so you keep this nice, smiling front. And after a while you are just going to explode. And if you don't explode, then you will be totally drained and the next day you will have to call in sick when you are not sick. That is what the burn-out syndrome is.

And if you become natural again I can guarantee you that you can work seventeen hours a day, seven days a week and you will be peppy. Sometimes you get sleepy but you won't get negative.

Learn to respect the five natural emotions and don't turn them into unnatural emotions. I will go very briefly through them.

We have only two natural **fears**: one of falling from high places, and the other one of unexpected loud noises. You can put a little child up here *(indicating the stage)* — any child — and he would not step down because he has a built-in fear of high places.

I am the death-and-dying lady and I am not afraid to die. But if somebody shot a bullet behind me, I would duck so fast that you would be surprised how fast I am.

These are the natural fears of high places and loud noises. You have been given them to keep you from harming your body — they help you to survive, literally.

(Turns to audience): What other fears do you have? *(amusement and silence from audience)* Say a few ones! *(repeats answers from audience)* Fear of death, what else? Failures. Respirators. Being alone. Rejection. Heights. The unknown. What the neighbors think. Snakes. Rats. Spiders. People *(giggles from audience)*. And so on.

You end up with a million unnatural fears that make life miserable, and then you pass your phobias on to your children and your children's children. As it is stated so beautifully in the Bible, "The sins of your fathers will be passed on to the children and the children's children." That is what is meant by original sin.

You have no idea how many people spend ninety percent of their life's energy and make choices in their daily life based on fear. That is the biggest, biggest problem you have. Because if you have a life without any fears except for the natural ones, you will be able to begin to live fully. In my workshops... you have no idea what kinds of decisions people make based on fear which they are totally unaware of. The fear of what the neighbors think has killed more children than anything else. The fear of not being loved, the fear of being rejected, the fear of not being a good girl or a good boy have caused more children to commit suicide than any other cause in the whole wide world. I want you to go home tonight, and if you have children, try to think for yourself privately: how many "ifs" do you attach to the statement "I love you."

People who have no fears of what the neighbors would say, people who have no fears of not being loved will live a whole, full life.

Very often when I'm standing at the casket of a child the parents say, "Why did I give him such a hard time? Why didn't I see the beauty of this child? Why did I complain that my son played the drums every night? I complained and complained. Tonight I would have given anything in the world to hear him play the drums."

Grief is a natural emotion and one of the greatest gifts that man is given to take care of all the losses in life. How many of you were allowed to cry as little children? If we would allow our children to grieve when they experience the thousand little deaths in their life, they would not end up as grownups full of self-pity. Our children are very often not allowed to grieve. *(Turns to audience):* What were you told when you were crying? *(repeats answers from audience):* "Big boys don't cry." "You are a cry baby." "Go to your room if you cry again." "God, here she goes again!" *(laughter of recognition from audience)* And my favorite, "If you don't stop crying, I will give you something to cry about!" *(laughter of recognition and applause)* Those children will have a tremendous problem later on with anything related to grief, and they often end up with buckets of self-pity.

If a child falls from a tricycle and you as a parent don't make a big fuss out of it but let her cry, then a few seconds later she will be up on her tricycle taking off again. In this way she will prepare herself for life's windstorms. She will not become a sissy. She will become strong because she will not have a pool of repressed tears.

Repressed grief turns into pulmonary problems and asthma. You can stop an asthmatic attack if you help the patient to cry. I am not saying that repressed grief by itself *causes* asthma, but a pool of re-pressed tears adds enormously to asthma, to pulmonary problems and to GI problems. If you have families with a big history of asthma and help them to get their tears out, they are going to be much bet-ter off.

Anger is even worse. Children are not supposed to be angry. But then the natural anger in a child that is raised naturally only takes fifteen seconds, which is long enough to say, "No, mom!"

(Turns to audience) How may of you were spanked, bashed, belted, punished or sent to your room when you were angry as a child? *(silence from audience)* Nobody here in Sweden? *(laughter)* I can't be-lieve that. How many of you were *not ever* punished when you were angry?

Very few children are accepted when they are angry. What the parents need to learn then is that natural anger only lasts for fifteen seconds. Then it's over with and they are ready to move on. But if you are not allowed to be angry and, even worse, if you get spanked, punished or reprimanded, then you will become Hitlers, small and big Hitlers, who are full of rage and revenge and hate. The world is full of them. And I'm using this word specifically because there is a Hitler in all of us. A mini-Hitler or a maxi-Hitler.

If you, as a grownup, have the courage to get in touch with your own repressed anger from way back since you were a child, and get in touch with how many times you have been mad at somebody or angry at somebody for more than fifteen seconds, then you will get in touch with something that has been repressed which we call rage, hate and revenge. This is physically the worst kind of unfinished business you can carry with you, because if you keep those repressed feelings inside of you for any extended period of time they will eventually affect your physical quadrant and will lead to ill health.

Hate, which is distorted anger, is a great killer in terms of physical illness. Every unnatural emotion has its physical equivalent: a coronary is an expression of repressed fear and anger. If you are a member of a family genetically inclined to coronaries at age forty and you are a man approaching that age and you know it's like a knife over your head, then come to one of my workshops and I will help you get rid of your anger and fear. You have never imagined what is inside of you — it is like a pressure cooker that is ready to erupt. Get rid of your fear and anger and in spite of the genetic probability of having a coronary at a young age you will add years to your life span. It is the repressed negative emotions that are the great killers in our society.

Billy

I once made a house call to an eight-year-old dying child. The parents were hovering over him and in the same room there was another little child sitting near the window all by himself like he didn't belong to the family. I presumed that he was a visiting neighbor. Nobody included him, nobody talked to him, nobody introduced him to me. It was like he was nonexistent. If you see the patients in their home you learn a lot. I too ignored him totally and played into the scheme of this family.

In the course of the conversation I realized that this must be Billy, the brother of the sick child. He was about seven years old. Before I left, I asked him to draw a picture and I realized that the dying boy had no problems but *he*, Billy, had more problems than the rest of the family together. I asked him what his big problem was and he couldn't tell me in plain English. I asked him to draw another picture, and then I was able to talk to him as a result of his own picture.

As I was leaving when my house call was finished I got up and said to Billy, "I want *you* to walk me to the door." He jumped up and said, "Me?" I said, "You, and you alone." And I gave the mother what I call the "eagle eye" *(laughter from audience)* which means, "You stay right where you are and you are not going to come out and snoop on what I'm doing with that little boy." She got the message and we walked to the door. And at the door he grabbed my hand, and just as he closed the door enough, not to be visible to the parents, he looked at me and said, "I guess you know that I have asthma." And I blurted out (I'm most of the time not thinking first), "That doesn't surprise me."

By then we were at the car and we sat in the front seat and we closed the door half way so the snooping parents couldn't peek.

I said, "So you have asthma!" And he said very sadly, "I guess it's not good enough." And I said, "Not good enough?" He said very matter of factly, "My brother gets electric train sets, he gets trips to Disneyland, there is nothing that they would not do for him. But when I wanted a football my dad said no. And when I asked him how come, he got very angry and said, 'Would you rather have cancer?'"

Do you understand the logical thinking of those parents? Do you understand the boy's tragedy?

Children take everything literally. It is no wonder that some children develop psychosomatic symptoms. If we, the grownups, tell them quite explicitly, "If you have cancer you can get anything, but if you are well, don't make any demands on us," then it is understandable that such a child will grow up with tremendous rage, hate, revenge and self-pity. He may think something like this, "If my brother gets bigger toys the more sick he gets, maybe I'm not sick enough, and I have to get more sick." That is the beginning of psychosomatic illness. Then he develops asthma, and the more sick he becomes, the bigger the gift he thinks that he will get. Later on, he may become a big, big manipulator because anytime he wants something he will have a dramatic heart attack or asthma attack.

He may also wish that his brother will die quickly so that life will become normal again and so that he will again get a little slice of the pie. That, of course, will make him feel very guilty.

We see this kind of unnatural behavior very often. You can help parents to understand that they have to really watch what they tell little children because they take everything so literally. And you can help this little child to grieve for all the things that he didn't get and also that he never got enough attention. He would be helped if he is allowed to grieve and if a neighbor or a clergyman or a friend or anybody takes this healthy little boy out and gives him special attention. They can do a lot of preventive medicine and preventive psychiatry by making him understand that he doesn't have to have cancer in order to be loved. All children need love, and if they get it they will not have to develop asthma in order to compete with a brother who has cancer.

It is quite a different thing with children who have been loved unconditionally and have been allowed to express their natural anger. When they are dying they will be able to tell you in a very few minutes when they have had enough of the treatment. Their intuitive quadrant knows when they are only going to live a few days more, and they will tell mommy or daddy or a doctor or a nurse, or someone else they trust, "It is time now for me to go home." If you can hear that, you will never miss the chance when the patient tells you, "I have a few days to live. I need to go home now." And you would love to hear that, and you would then easily find the courage to stop the chemotherapy or whatever it is you have initiated, because you would already know that the patient knows that he is not going to live through it.

The beauty in working with dying patients — if you are ready to get rid of your own blocks, your own unfinished business — is that you will be able to *hear* the intuitive quadrant of your patient speaking. In all my twenty years of working with dying patients, grownups and children, I have never had a patient who did not know that he was dying. That includes five-year-old children, who, from the intellectual quadrant, have no idea what is wrong with them. Still they can tell you not only what is wrong with them — not in scientific language but in drawings — but they also can tell you when death is near. *If* you can hear that, *if* the parents do not project their own needs, *if* the doctor allows himself to that patients know more about themselves than he does, then you will never have a problem with the artificial prolongation of life when it is not helpful. I will give you a very practical example of that when I have finished talking about the natural emotions.

Jealousy is a natural emotion, very natural, very positive. It helps little children to emulate, to copy older children learning how to ski, ice skate, play the flute, read a book. If you belittle them in their natural jealousy, it turns into very ugly envy and competition. If this form of natural jealousy is knocked and belittled, it turns the mind into a state of an unending competition.

Love is the biggest problem of them all, a problem that pushes our world almost to self-destruction. If we do not understand love, we run into problems, not only with dying patients but also with the living. Love consists of two aspects. One of them is holding, hugging, touching, and giving physical security. And the other one, the most important part that is forgotten by most people, is the courage to say "no;" to say "NO" in capital letters to somebody you love. If you cannot say no, it is a sign that you have too much fear, shame or guilt within you. A mother who ties shoelaces for her child until he is twelve years old doesn't give him love but the opposite because she cannot say "no" to him.

There is also another way of saying "no" that parents have to learn. Parents who love a child *so* much that they don't let him cross the street by himself and don't let him stay away with friends over-night and don't allow him to go anywhere, those parents have not learned to say "no" to *their own* needs. They do not express love for their child by stopping him. On the contrary, they project their own fears and their own unfinished business onto him.

If you have too much fear, shame and guilt to say "no" to your children or to yourself, you will raise a generation of cripples, de-priving them from living, and depriving yourself of the greatest experience of your life.

Jeffy

When you work with dying children, you experience what the effects of lack of love are all about. And you go home and look at your own children and try to practice what dying children teach you. My best and briefest example is nine-year-old Jeffy, who had leukemia for six out of his nine years in life. He was in and out of the hospital. He was a very sick boy when I saw him for the last time in the hospital. He had central nervous system involvement. He was like a drunk little man. His skin was very pale, almost discolored. He was barely able to stand on his feet. He had lost his hair many, many times with chemotherapy. He could not even look at the injection needles any more, and everything was too painful for him.

I was very aware that this child had a few weeks, at the most, to live. After you take care of a family with such a child for six years out of his nine years, you naturally become part of it.

That very day it was a very young, new physician who came on his rounds. As I walked in I heard him say to Jeffy's parents, "We are going to try another chemotherapy."

I asked the parents and the physicians if they had asked Jeffy, if *he* was willing to take another series of treatment. As the parents loved him unconditionally, they were able to allow me to ask this question to Jeffy in their presence. Jeffy gave me a most beautiful answer in the way children speak. He very simply said, "I don't understand you grownups, why you have to make us children so sick to get us well?"

We talked about it. This was Jeffy's way of expressing the natural fifteen seconds of anger. This child had enough self-worth, inner authority and self-love to have the courage to say, "No thank you," which was what Jeffy said. The parents were able to hear it, respect it and accept it.

Then I wanted to say good-bye to Jeffy. But Jeffy said, "No. I want to be sure that I am taken home today." If a child tells you, "Take me home *today*," there is a sense of great urgency, and we try *not* to postpone it. Therefore I asked the parents if they were willing to take him home. The parents had enough love and courage to do that.

And again I wanted to say good bye. But Jeffy, like all children who are still terribly honest and simple, said to me, "I want *you* to come home with me."

I looked at my watch, which in the symbolic, nonverbal language means, "You know, I really don't have the time to go home with all my children." Without my saying anything in words, he understood instantly and said, "don't worry, it will only take ten minutes."

I went home with him, knowing that in the next ten minutes at home Jeffy would finish his unfinished business. We drove home — the parents, Jeffy and I. We drove into the driveway, opening the garage.

We are in the garage and get out of the car. Jeffy says very matter-of-factly to his father, "Take my bicycle down from the wall."

Jeffy had a brand new bicycle that was hanging on two hooks inside the garage wall. For a long time the dream of his life had been to be able, once in his lifetime, to ride around the block on a bicycle. And so his father had bought him a beautiful bicycle. But because of his illness he had never been able to ride it. It had been hanging there on its hooks for three years.

Now Jeffy asked his dad to take it down. With tears in his eyes he asked him to put the training wheels on the bicycle. I do not know if you appreciate how much humility it takes for a nine-year-old boy to ask for training wheels, usually used only by very little children.

And the father, with tears in his eyes, put the training wheels on his son's bicycle. Jeffy was like a drunk man, barely able to stand on his feet.

When the father was finished with the training wheels, Jeffy took one look at me and said, "And *you* Doctor Ross, you are here to hold my mom back."

Jeffy knew that his mom had one problem, one unfinished business. She was not yet able to learn the love that can say "no" to her own needs. Her biggest need was to lift up her very sick child on the bicycle like a two-year-old, to hold onto him and to run with him around the block. And thus she would have cheated him out of the greatest victory of his life.

Therefore I held mom back, and her husband held *me* back. We held each other back and learned the hard way how painful and difficult it sometimes is in the face of a very vulnerable, terminally ill child to allow him the victory and the risk to fall and hurt and bleed.

He drove off.

After an eternity he came back, the proudest man you have ever seen. He was beaming from one ear to the other. He looked like somebody who had won the gold medal in the Olympics.

He very proudly came off the bicycle and asked his father with *great* authority and sense of pride to take the training wheels off and to carry the bicycle into his bedroom.

And then very unsentimentally, very beautifully, very straight-forwardly he turned to me and said, "And you, Dr. Ross, you can go home now." He kept his promise that it would only take ten minutes of my time.

But he also gave me the greatest gift that I was able to witness: his great victory, the fulfillment of an incredible dream. This would *never* have been possible had we kept him in the hospital.

Two weeks later his mother called me up and said, "I have to tell you the end of the story."

After I had left, Jeffy said, "When my brother comes home from school" — his brother was Dougy, a first grader — "you send him upstairs, but no grown-ups, please." That is again the "no thank you." And they respected that.

Dougy came home and was sent up to his brother. When he, a while later, came down again, he refused to tell his parents what he and his brother had been talking about.

It was only two weeks later that he was allowed to tell us what had happened during that visit.

Jeff had told Dougy that he wanted the pleasure of personally giving him his most beloved bicycle. But he could not wait another two weeks until it was Dougy's birthday, because by then he would be dead. Therefore he wanted to give it to him now, but only under one condition: that Dougy would *never* use those damned training wheels *(laughter from audience)*. This was another expression of fif-teen seconds of anger.

Jeffy died a week later. Dougy had his birthday another week later and was then allowed to share with us the end of the story: how a nine-year-old child finished his unfinished business.

And I hope you realize that the parents had a lot of grief, but no grief *work*, no fear, no guilt, no shame, "Oh my God, if we had only been able and willing to hear him."

They had the memory of this ride around the block and that beaming face of Jeffy, who was able to achieve his great victory over something that most of us, unfortunately, take all too for granted.

Children know what they need. Children know when the time is close. Children share with you their unfinished business. And it is only your own fear and your own guilt and your own shame and your own clinging on that prevents you from hearing it. And by doing so you cheat yourself out of sacred moments like this one.

My next brief example of unfinished business has nothing to do with hate or unresolved grief work. It has to do with taking the good things for granted... *(interrupts herself)* By the way, how many of you have not talked to your mother-in-law for ten years or more? *(amusement in audience)* I do not expect public confessions *(laughter)* but at least ask yourself: why do I treat people who don't approve of me... why do I need to treat them with the revenge of silence?

If that mother-in-law of yours dies tomorrow, you will spend a fortune at the florist, and that only helps the florist *(laughter)*. But if tomorrow you feel that ten years of punishment is enough, then you may go and pick some flowers and give them to her. But do not expect her to love you or thank you. She may even throw them in your face, but *you* will have given her your peace offering. If she then dies the next day you will have grief but no grief work. Grief is natural and a God-given gift. Grief work is, "If I had only . . ."

But unfinished business is not only unexpressed grief, anger, jealousy, and negative things. Unfinished business can bother you just as much if you have had positive experiences which you have not shared with your fellow man. A teacher, for example, who has been very influential in your life and has really given your life sense and purpose and direction, and you never took the time to say thank you to him, and then suddenly he dies and you think, "God, it would have been nice if I had written him a letter."

Maybe the best and briefest example of this kind of unfinished business which can haunt you for years and years afterwards is a letter that a young girl wrote about Viet Nam. It is an "If I had only...":

Remember the day I borrowed your brand new car and I dented it?

I thought you'd kill me, but you didn't.

Remember the time I dragged you to the beach and you said it would rain and it did?

I thought you'd say, "I told you so," but you didn't.

Remember the time I flirted with all the guys to make you jealous and you were?

I thought that you'd leave me, but you didn't.

And the time I spilled blueberry pie over your brand new trousers?

I thought you'd drop me for sure, but you didn't.

And the time I forgot to tell you the dance was formal and you showed up in blue jeans?

I thought you'd smack me, but you didn't.

There were so many things that I wanted to make up to you when you returned from Viet Nam.

But you didn't.

I hope that if you have had a Grandma or a kindergarten teacher or anybody who was really special to you — it doesn't have to be in your family — that you say all these things before you hear that he or she has died. That too is unfinished business.

When you take the courage to become honest again, as honest as children are, you will begin to see that you have the courage to evaluate and to look honestly on your own unfinished business. Get rid of it so that you can become whole again. Then your intuitive, spiritual quadrant will emerge. You don't have to do anything for it except to get rid of your negativity. When you have developed this, your life will change drastically.

You will then always hear your patients. You will always hear when they need help. You will always hear from *whom* they need help — this is not always you. You will also hear what it is that they need in order to finish whatever they have not yet finished.

Working with dying patients then becomes an incredible blessing. And it will never ever lead to a burn-out, because each time you react, each time you find some little unfinished business popping up from time to time like a weed in the garden, you will know that you have to weed your garden again.

When you finish your unfinished business, all your repressed hate and greed and grief work and all the negative stuff that ruins not only your life, but also your health, you will find that it no longer matters whether you die at twenty or fifty or ninety, and then you will have nothing to be worried about.

When you discover that same source of inner knowledge within other people, with people who die a sudden death, you will find that even children who have been murdered, even children who are hit by a car and die a sudden, unexpected death, know inside not only *that* they will die but also *how* they will die.

It is important that you know that the younger you are the more you know. The less you know up here *(indicating head)* the more you know here *(indicating intuitive quadrant)* — almost, it is not totally so. And people who are intellectually hypertrophic... Do you understand what I mean by that? You go to school for years and years and years and in that process you lose your intuition, because you learn to analyze everything up here *(head)*, and you forget that you know far more in here *(intuition)*. You get into trouble with your intellectual quadrant and you need to really learn how to keep it in harmony with your intuitive quadrant. That is very difficult.

Do you hear what I am trying to say to you? Finishing your own unfinished business is the only way that you can bring about a change in the world. And I will briefly talk as a psychiatrist because it is very important that you heal the world soon, before it is too late: *you have to understand that you cannot heal the world without healing yourself first.*

❦

(A man in the audience asks a question.) Did everybody hear the question? *("No!")* He asked how we can deal with conflicts with the society, how the society could work with dying patients, so that we don't have to work only on an individual level like I do. *You* are the society! In 1968, I was the only person who talked to dying patients in the United States and who taught it in medical schools and theological seminaries. And in the last years we have had 125,000 courses every year in the United States alone. It starts with one person, and you can start it. You have started it already.

We had one hospice in 1970. And last year we had 100 hospices coming up in one year in California alone. They are coming up like "Chicken Delights." I hope you understand what I mean. This is not good. It is very *en vogue* right now. Everybody starts hospices because they get government money, and it's politically wise to do it. But if something is not done out of love, unconditional love, but instead out of profit or prestige or as an ego trip, then it is not worth it. So if ten thousand people here in Sweden start having the courage to take the patients home to die, helping your neighbors to take their husband or their child home, then it would take very few people to do this work. And as long as you do it free of charge, without expectations of starting a famous "Death & Dying Center" or whatever non-positive motivations you might have, you will do a wonderful job with your dying patients. It takes one or two people who are not afraid to start it. And you may experience a lot of abuse, and a lot of hostility at some times, but the fruit of your labor is worthwhile. That is really all I can say about it.

<hr />

(Question from audience, "What do you say to a child whose mother has committed suicide?") We see many children whose mothers have committed suicide. You do not preach to them, you do not say anything *to* them. You let the child draw a picture and let him share with you what it means to him, and give him a safe place where he can externalize his rage, his anger, his sense of unfairness, and his tremendous grief. And then, when he has poured out all that anguish and anger, only then we begin to help him to understand why some

people find this the only solution. And we do it with compassion. Not with judgment.

But you cannot do that until you have helped him to externalize his rage, his impotence, his anger, and for this you need a very safe place. That is what we do in our workshops. All people in our workshops have pains like that.

(Elisabeth invites the audience to ask more questions specifically about children and death before she will move on to the next subject for the evening which is life after death. Nevertheless, a lot of people in the audience start asking questions about life after death. For a while though, she only answers questions about children and death and the audience becomes more and more impatient to hear about life after death. Elisabeth picks up these feelings from the audience and the following is her response to those feelings.)

(Impatient question from audience, "When are you going to talk about life after death?" Elisabeth answers.)

As soon as the earthly business is finished *(reluctant laughs fro m audience).*

There are a lot of people who want to know a lot about life after death and they do not understand that if you live fully and in harmony, without negativity and without unfinished business, you will get *your own* experiences. To live this way is the only way to become totally open on the intuitive and spiritual quadrant. I have never myself done *anything* to achieve all my mystical experiences. I can't even sit still to meditate. I eat meat, I drink coffee, I smoke, I have never been to India, I don't have a Guru or a Baba *(laughs from audience)* and I have had every... *(applause)* ... and I have had every mystical experience that you could ever dream of ever getting in your life.

And the only thing that I would like to convey to you is that you do not need drugs, you do not need to go to India, you do not need a Guru or a Baba or outside people who tell you how to do it. If you are ready for spiritual experiences and you are not afraid you will get them yourself.

If you are not ready for them, you will not believe what I tell you. But on the other hand, if you *know* already, then they could hang you by your toe nails and still you would know.

Do you see the difference between *knowing* something and *believing* something? Once you know, no matter what they do to you, you will know that death does not exist. I have collected twenty-thousand cases of near death experiences and I stopped collecting them because I had the illusion that it was my job to tell people that death does not exist.

I believed that it was of utmost importance to tell people what happens at the moment of death, and I discovered very soon *(with just a hint of pain in her voice)* — and the price wasn't terribly low — that those who are ready to listen know it anyway, just the way my children — when they are ready for it — know that they are dying. On the other hand, those who do *not* believe it, those people you could give one-million examples and they would *still* tell you it's only a result of oxygen deprivation. But this doesn't really matter because after they die, they will know it anyway *(amusement, giggles and applause from audience)*. If they need to rationalize those things away, that is their problem.

The only Hitler I want to keep inside of me is that when those people who gave me a hard time as a result of publicly speaking about the near-death experience, make the transition, I am gonna to sit there, and I'm gonna watch their surprised faces, and I'm gonna... *(laughter from audience)* ... use symbolic, nonverbal language! *(laughter and applause)*

I'm going to tell you now anyway what you need to know, if it helps.

It is very important to me that people who do research on life after death do it in as systematic and as scientific a way as there is. Because if you don't use the right language, it sounds very coo-coo.

I have worked with dying patients for the last twenty years and when I started this work I must say that I was neither very interested in life after death nor did I have any really clear picture of the definition of death except naturally for those that the science of medicine has defined. When you study the definition of death, you see that it only includes the death of the physical body as if man only consisted of the cocoon.

I was one of those physicians, scientists, who did not ever question that. But in the 1960s it started to become very difficult to be a physician with the transplants coming and the deep freeze societies and people believing that we can conquer death with money and technology. They froze people at the moment of death and promised to defrost them "twenty years from now" when there might be a cure for cancer. People spent $9,000 a year with the illusion that their next of kin could be defrosted alive. It was like the peak of arrogance and stupidity, if you don't mind my saying so. It was ignorance, grandiosity, a denial of our own mortality, a denial of the origin from where we came. It was a denial that life has a purpose, and that life in this physical world does not *have* to last forever, it was a denial of the fact that the quality of life is far more important than the years — the quantity of life.

And in those days it became extremely difficult to be a physician because in the United States... I remember one day when we had twelve parents in the waiting room for *one* child to be saved. We had to dialyze in those days, but we didn't have enough equipment, and physicians had to choose only one out of twelve children for dialysis. Which one deserved most to live?

It was a terrible nightmare.

Then they also came up with liver transplants and heart transplants and even started to talk about brain transplants. And in parallel the law suits started to come in, since our materialism has reached a point where people sue each other where the issue of prolongation has raised many, many difficult problems. Also we can be sued for either attempting to take an organ too early out of a person when the family claims that they are still alive, or when we wait too long and perhaps often prolong the life unnecessarily.

The life insurance companies have also added to this problem in that in a family accident it is sometimes of vital importance to know who in a family died first, even if it is only a matter of minutes. Again the issue is money and who the beneficiaries would be.

Needless to say, all these issues would have touched me very little had it not been for my own very subjective experiences at the bedside of my own dying patients. Being a skeptical semi-believer to put it mildly, and not interested in issues of life after death, I could not help but be impressed by several observations which occurred so frequently that I began to wonder why nobody ever had studied the *real* issues of death — not for any special scientific reasons, not to cover lawsuits, needless to say, but simply out of sheer natural curiosity.

One day, when several lawsuits had come into the hospital, I had a discussion with the beautiful black minister with whom I started the old Death and Dying seminars at the University of Chicago. I loved him very dearly, and with him I had had this super-ideal symbiosis. This day he philosophized with me on what we could do to bring medicine back to where it used to be. And I was an old fashioned country doctor from Switzerland so I had lots of ideals about my profession. And we decided that the real problem was that we don't have a definition of death.

Man has existed for forty-seven million years and has been in his present existence, which includes the facet of divinity, for seven million years. Every day people die all over the world and yet in a society that is able to send a man to the moon and bring him back alive and safe, we have never put any efforts into the study of an updated and total definition of human death. Isn't that peculiar?

We have definitions, but they all have exceptions, like if you have barbiturates or if you are very cold you can have a flat EEG and can still be brought back to a normal life without brain damage. And any definition that has exceptions is obviously not the final definition. And so in my juvenile enthusiasm I said to this minister, "I'm going to promise God that I live long enough to find a definition of death." It was a very naive, childlike fantasy to think that if we had a definition of death then the lawsuits would disappear and we could go back to being healers and physicians.

And because I always had lots of problems with other ministers who talk a lot and don't believe what they are saying and don't live it themselves, I challenged this one and said, "You guys, you are always up on the pulpit and you say 'Ask and you will be given'. I'm gonna ask you now: help me to do research on death."

The Near-Death Experience

It is said somewhere, "Ask and you will be given. Knock and it will be open." Or, in a different language, "A teacher will appear when the student is ready." This proved to be very true. Within one week after raising this important question and making a commitment to finding an answer to it, we were visited by nurses who shared with us the experience of a woman, a Mrs. Schwartz, who had been in the intensive care unit fifteen times.

Each time this woman was expected to die, and yet each time she was able to walk out of the intensive care unit to live for another few weeks or months. She was, as we would call it now, our first case of a near-death experience.

This occurred simultaneously with my increasing sensitivity and observation of other unexplained phenomena at the time when my own patients were very, very close to death. Many of them began to "hallucinate" the presence of loved ones with whom they apparently had some form of communication but whom I, personally, was neither able to see nor hear.

I was also quite aware that even the angriest and most difficult patients, very shortly before death, begin to deeply relax, have a sense of serenity around them, and begin to be pain free in spite of, perhaps, a cancer-ridden body full of metastases. Also, at the moment after death, their facial features expressed an incredible sense of peace and equanimity and serenity which I could not comprehend since it was often a death that occurred during a stage of anger, bargaining or depression.

My third and perhaps most subjective observation was the fact that I have always been very close to my patients and allowed myself to get deeply and lovingly involved with them. They touched my life and I touched their lives in a very intimate, meaningful way. Yet within minutes after the death of a patient I had no feelings for him or her, and I often wondered if there was something wrong with me. When I looked at the body, it appeared to me similar to a winter coat, shed with the occurrence of spring, not needed any more. I had this incredible, clear image of a shell, and my beloved patient was no longer in there.

We discovered that it is possible to do research on life after death. This discovery was, for me, an incredibly moving experience, and I will simply summarize what we have learned in the last many, many years, studying this phenomenon, which is called — for the time being — the near-death experience.

Our dream was to collect twenty cases. We have now twenty-thousand cases. We never published them and I'm glad we never did because what we found out when we started to look for cases was that there were lots of people who were willing to share with us, but they always started their sharing by saying, "Dr. Ross, I will share something with you if you promise not to tell it to another human being." They were almost paranoid about it. Because when they came back after having had this glorious experience which for them was very sacred, very private, and shared it with people, they got a nice little pat on their back and were told, "Well, you were under drugs," or "It is very normal that people hallucinate at moments like this."

They were also given psychiatric labels which, of course, made them very angry or depressed. We always need to label things that we don't understand. There are many things that we don't know yet. But that doesn't mean that they don't exist.

We collected these cases not only from the United States but also Australia and Canada; the youngest patient is a two-year-old child, the oldest a ninety-seven year old man. We have people from different cultural and religious backgrounds including Eskimos, original Hawaiians, aborigines from Australia, Hindus, Buddhists, Protestants, Catholics, Jews, and several people without any religious identification, including a few who called themselves agnostics or atheists. It was important for us to collect data from the greatest possible variety of people from different religious and cultural backgrounds, as we wanted to be very sure not only that our material was not contaminated, but that it was a uniquely *human* experience, and that it had nothing to do with early conditioning, religious or otherwise.

Also relevant is the fact that they had these experiences after an accident, murder attempt, suicide attempt or a slow lingering death. Over half of our cases have been sudden death experiences. In these cases the patients have not been able to prepare themselves for, or anticipate, an experience.

Whoever among you is ready to hear the truth will not have to look far in order to get your own cases. If children sense your motivation, they will share their knowledge freely. But if you are out to be negative, they will pick it up very quickly and they will not share anything with you. I am not exaggerating when I say to you: If you can get rid of your own negativity, then everything will be open for you and the patients will sense it, and they will share with you. And you will find that they will give you all the knowledge that you need, that you are ready for — but not more. And you know, some of you are in high school and some of you are only in first grade. You will always get what you need, but you will not always get what you want. That is a universal law.

<hr>

We say that you are not really you, the way you look at yourself in the mirror and the way you worry every day that you are too fat or too flat-chested or your hips are to fat or you have too many wrinkles. That is *totally* irrelevant. You are beautiful because you are you, because you are unique. There are billions of people and no two are alike. Not even identical triplets. And I am an identical triplet *(she laughs a little)*.

In memory of the children in Auschwitz and Maidanek, we are using the model of the cocoon and the butterfly. We say that you are like the cocoon of a butterfly. The cocoon is what you see in a mirror. It is only a temporary housing of your *real* you. When this cocoon gets damaged beyond repair, you die, and what happens is that the cocoon, which is created of physical energy, will — symbolically speaking — relieve the butterfly.

You have the same subjective experience of death whether the destruction of the cocoon happens through homicide, suicide, sudden death or slow lingering death. The cause of death does not alter the subjective experience of the moment of death.

The immortal part of you will be released out of your physical shell. What you bury or cremate is not you, it's only the cocoon.

That is very important to understand. When we work with little children, we show them how this happens. At that moment you will be very beautiful. Much more beautiful than you see yourself now. You will be perfect. Mutilations like mastectomies and amputations do not follow you into death. But the body you now have is no longer created by physical energy but psychic energy.

The Common Denominators

We will share with you the three common denominators that we have found.

When we leave the physical body there will be a total absence of panic, fear or anxiety. We will have all awareness. Awareness is higher than consciousness because it also includes everything that's going on in the environment where our physical body is shed: what people in the vicinity of our body are thinking, what kind of excuses they use to lie to themselves and things like that.

We will always experience a physical wholeness. We will be totally aware of the environment in which the accident or death takes place, whether this is a hospital room, our own bedroom after a coronary, or the scene of a car accident or a plane crash. We will be quite aware of the people who work in the resuscitation team or the rescue team trying to extricate the body from a car wreck. We will watch this at a distance of a few feet in a rather detached state of mind, if I may use the word "mind," though we are no longer connected with the mind or with a functioning brain at this moment in most cases. This all occurs at a time when brain-wave tests give no signs of brain activities, and very often at the time when physicians find no signs of life whatsoever.

Our second body, which we experience at this time, is not a physical body, but an ethereal body, and we will talk later on about the differences between physical, psychic and spiritual energy, which create these forms.

It is understandable that many of our patients who have been successfully resuscitated are not always grateful when their butterfly is squashed back into the cocoon, since with the revival of our bodily functions we also have to accept the pains and the handicaps that go with it.

In the state of the ethereal body we have no pain and no handicaps. Many of my colleagues wondered if this is not simply a projection of our wishful thinking, which would be very understandable and comprehensible. If anyone has been paralyzed, mute, blind or handicapped for many years, they may be looking forward to a time when the suffering is ended. But it is very easy to evaluate whether this is a projection of wishful thinking or not.

Number one: half of our cases have been sudden, unexpected accidents or near-death experiences where people were unable to foresee what was going to hit them, as in the case of a hit-and-run driver who amputated the legs of one of our patients. And yet, when he was out of his physical body, he saw his amputated leg on the highway and at the same time was fully aware of having both of his legs on his ethereal, perfect and whole body. So we cannot assume that he had previous knowledge of the loss of his legs and would therefore project, in his own wishful thinking, that he was able to walk again.

Number two: there is also a much simpler way to rule out the projection of wishful thinking. That is to ask blind people who do not even have light perception to share with us what it was like when they had this near death experience. If it were just a dream fulfillment those people would not be able to give accurate details of their surroundings.

We have questioned several totally blind people who were able to share with us in their near death experience and they were not only able to tell us who came into the room first, who worked on the resuscitation, but they were also able to give minute details of the attire and the clothing of all the people present, something a totally blind person, the victim of wishful thinking, would never be able to do.

You need to understand that this is not the resurrection that is described in Christian teaching. The body we have during a near death experience is a very temporary form, created out of psychic energy to help you make the experience of death a pleasant reunion, and not a scary, frightening, horrifying experience.

Once we have gone through something that symbolizes a transition — it is culturally determined and can be a gate or a bridge or a
tunnel — we begin to see a light. It is a light that is beyond any
description. It is whiter than white, lighter than light, and when we
come closer to it, we will be totally wrapped in unconditional love.
If we have ever, ever, ever experienced that, we can never, ever again
be afraid of death. Death is not scary. It is what we make out of life
that is the problem.

People who have seen this light have for, a glimpse of a moment,
all knowledge. Unfortunately, if they have to come back — if it is a
near death experience — they forget a lot of it. But what many of
them remember is, I think, the only thing that we should be aware
of, and that is that our total life is our own responsibility, that we
cannot criticize and blame and judge and hate. We, and we alone
are responsible for the sum total of our physical life. That realiza-
tion changes a lot of our priorities.

In the presence of this incredible light, which people call "Christ"
or "God" or "Love" or "Light" depending on where they come from,
we will be held responsible for everything we have done. And we
will then understand how often we have not taken the highest choice
and how we have suffered the consequences of our choices.

Here we will know that the absolutely only thing that matters is
love. Everything else, our achievements, degrees, the money we
made, how many mink coats we had, is totally irrelevant. It will
also be understood that *what* we do is not important. The only thing
that matters is *how* we do what we do. And the only thing that matters is that we do what we do with love.

In this total, unconditional love we will have to review not only
every deed of our life, but also every thought and every word of
our total existence. And we will have all knowledge. That means
that we will know how every thought, word and deed and choice
of our total life has affected others. Our life is literally nothing but a
school, where we are tested, where we are put through the tumbler.
And it is *our* choice, and no one else's choice, whether we come out
of the tumbler crushed or polished.

You can collect thousands of cases of near-death experiences — if you need to. But we became very aware that it is not necessary to do that. Because those who want to believe will believe, those who want to know will find out — if they so wish — and those who are not ready for it — if you have a hundred-and-fifty-thousand cases, they will come up with a hundred-and-fifty- thousand rationalizations. And that is their problem.

What I need to say before I end is that Moody's first book, *Life after Life*, which is the only one that is correct, is helpful, but it will not tell you what death is all about, because those are all *near*-death experiences.

After we shed our physical body, which is *physical* energy, we create a secondary, perfect body — meaning without blindness, without amputations, without mastectomies, without defects — with *psychic* energy, which is man-created and manipulated by man, by our mind.

When we are permanently dead, if I can use such horrible language, irreversibly dead, then we will take on a different form that is the form that we have before birth and after death. And that is when we, in Moody's language, go through the tunnel toward the light. That light is pure *spiritual* energy. Spiritual energy is the only energy form in this Universe that cannot be manipulated by man.

<hr>

Those of you who do research in this field or study higher consciousness or want to understand more about the intricate design of life have to learn two essential things. The first thing is the difference between *real* and *reality*. And the second is the differences between physical, psychic and spiritual energy. Because you are going to read papers by scientists who share with you the existence of Satan and of Hell and of nightmarish and scary and very real nightmares that especially coronary patients, who are frightened, experience. Those nightmares are *real* but not *reality*. They are projections of one's own fears and are very real but not reality.

Psychic energy is, as I mentioned, the creation of man. It is meant as a gift, and it is up to you to turn this gift into nightmares and ugly negative things or into blessings. Use your psychic energy to learn how to heal and do not use it to destroy.

Voodoo death is a classical example of using psychic energy to kill those who are afraid of the curse of voodoo. I can kill anybody, if I choose, with psychic energy, with voodoo death, if he is afraid of voodoo. But on the other hand, if all of you would put a curse on me with your own psychic energy, which is very powerful, all your psychic energy in this room could not touch me as long as I have no fear of voodoo. Negativity can only feed on negativity. Raise your children without fear and guilt and help them to get rid of the Hitler in them, so you can create Mother Theresas.

If you are honest again and become like children, you will learn that all it takes is to honestly look at yourself and your own negativity. If you have the courage to get rid of that negativity, you will then become whole, and you will learn unconditional love and discipline. As you practice that and learn that, you will be able to teach it and pass it on to your children.

I think Richard Allen put this very beautifully when he summed up not his own life but the life of his father. His father was to him an example of a man who started very negatively and struggled to get rid of his own negativity and his judgmental attitude and who became a being of total and unconditional love, able to pass it on to his children and his children's children. At the end of his life Richard wrote this poem about the meaning of life:

> When you love, give it everything you have got.
> And when you have reached your limit, give it more,
> and forget the pain of it.
> Because as you face your death
> it is only the love that you have given and received
> which will count,
> and all the rest:
> the accomplishments, the struggle, the fights
> will be forgotten in your reflection.
> And if you have loved well
> then it will all have been worth it.
> And the joy of it will last you through the end.

But if you have not,
death will always come too soon
and be too terrible to face.

I would like to finish with a prayer that is very interdenomina-
tional because it was written by American Indians to show you that
we are all brothers and sisters. It is a poem that was written hundreds of years ago. It is as true today as it will be in thousands of
years in the future.

Let me walk in beauty
and make my eyes ever behold
the red and purple sunset.
Make my hands respect the things you have made,
and my ears sharp to hear your voice.
Make me wise so that I may understand
the things you have taught my people.
Let me learn the lessons you have hidden
in every leaf and rock.
I seek strength
not to be greater than my brother
but to fight my greatest enemy:
myself.
Make me always ready to come to you
with clean hands and straight eyes.
So when life fades
as a fading sunset
my spirit may come to you without shame.

Thank you.

Elisabeth Kübler-Ross with Ndebele women (South Africa, January 1994)

Elisabeth Kübler-Ross in Egypt (Aswan, 1980)

Life, Death & Life After Death

I am sharing with you some of the experiences and findings that we have had during the last decade since we started to seriously study the whole issue of death and life after death. After working with patients for so many years it became very evident that in spite of our existence for so many millions of years as human beings we have not yet come to a clear understanding of perhaps the most important question of them all; namely the definition, meaning and purpose of life and death.

I wanted to share with you some of this research in death and life after death. I think that the time has come when we are all trying to put these findings together in a language that can help people to understand and also, perhaps, help them in dealing with the death of a loved one, especially the tragic occurrence of a sudden death when we don't quite understand why these tragedies have to happen to us. It is also very important when you try to counsel and help dying patients and their families and the question occurs over and over again: What is life? What is death? And why do children, especially young children, have to die?

We have not published any of our research, and that is for many reasons. We have studied near-death experiences for decades, but we were very aware that those were only *near* death experiences and that what we had were half-truths until we also knew what happens to people after they made the transition. The only thing that Shanti Nilaya has published so far is a letter that I wrote and illustrated in response to nine-year old Dougy with cancer from the southern parts of the United States who wrote me a very moving question, "What is life and what is death and why do young children have to die?" I wrote him a little letter in simple language, illustrated it, and sent it off to him. Later he gave us permission to have it printed and now *The Dougy Letter* is available from Shanti

Nilaya to help other young children to understand this most important question.

A long time ago people were much more in touch with the issue of death and believed in Heaven and life after death. It is only in the last hundred years, perhaps, that fewer and fewer people truly know that life exists after our physical body dies. There is no purpose to analyze it at this time and point out why this has occurred. But we are now in a new age and hopefully we have made the transition from an age of science and technology and materialism into a new age of genuine and authentic spirituality. This does not really mean religiosity but spirituality — an awareness that there is something far greater than we are, something that created this universe, created life; that we are an authentic and important and significant part of it, and that we can contribute to its evolution.

All of us, when we were born from the source, from God, have been endowed with this facet of divinity, and that means in a very literal sense that we have a part of that source within us. And that gives us the knowledge of our immortality. Many people are beginning to be aware that the physical body is only the house, or the temple, or — as we call it — the cocoon, which we inherit for a certain number of months or years, until we make the transition called death. Then, at the time of death, we shed this cocoon and we are again as free as butterflies, to use the symbolic language that we use when we talk to dying children and their siblings.

Mrs. Schwartz

One of my patients helped me to find out how to begin research into finding out what death really is and with it, naturally, the question of life after death. Mrs. Schwartz had been in and out of the intensive care unit fifteen times. Each time she was expected not to survive, and each time she managed to come back. Her husband was a known schizophrenic and each time he had a psychotic episode he tried to kill his youngest son, the youngest of many children. This son was not yet of age and he was the only one still at home. It was the patient's conviction that if she should die prematurely, her husband would lose control, and the life of her youngest son would be in danger. With the help of the Little Aid Society we were able to make arrangements for her to transfer the custody of this child to some relatives. She left the hospital with a great sense of relief and a new freedom, knowing that should she not be able to live long enough, at least her youngest child would be safe.

On one occasion when she became critically ill, she could not get to Chicago where she lived, and was, therefore, admitted to a local hospital in Indiana on an emergency basis.

She remembers being put in a private room. She suddenly sensed that she was only moments away from death, but she could not make up her mind whether she should call the nurse or not. One part of her wanted very much to lean back in the pillows and finally be at peace. But the other part of her needed to make it through one more time, because her youngest son was not yet of age. Before she made the decision to call the nurse and go through this whole rigmarole once more, a nurse apparently walked into her room, took one look at her and dashed out. At this very moment she saw herself slowly and peacefully floating out of her physical body and floating a few feet above her bed. She even had a great sense of humor, relating that she her body looked pale and icky. She had a sense of awe and surprise but no fear or anxiety.

She then watched the resuscitation team walk into the room and was able to enumerate in great detail who walked in first, who walked in last. She was totally aware, not only of every word of their conversations, but also of their thought patterns. She even repeated a joke that one of the residents who apparently was very apprehensive started to tell. She had only one great need, namely to tell them to relax, to take it easy, and that she was all right. But the more desperately she tried to convey it, the more frantically they seemed to work on her body until it dawned on her that she was able to perceive them but they were not able to perceive her. Mrs. Schwartz then decided to give up her attempts and, in her own words, "lost consciousness." She was declared dead after forty-five minutes of unsuccessful resuscitation attempts. Three and a half hours later she showed signs of life again, much to the surprise of the hospital staff. She lived another year and a half.

When Mrs. Schwartz shared this with me and my class in our seminar, it was a brand new experience to me. I had never heard of near-death experiences in spite of the fact that I had been a physician for many years. My students were shocked that I did not call this a hallucination, an illusion or a feeling of depersonalization. They had a desperate need to give it a label, something that they could identify with and then put aside, so as not to have to deal with it.

Mrs. Schwartz's experience, we were sure, could not be a single, unique occurrence. Our hope was to be able to find more cases like this and, perhaps, to go in the direction of collecting data to see if the experience that this patient had had was a common, rare, or very unique. The near death experience has now become known all over the world. Many, many researchers, physicians, psychologists and people who study parapsychological phenomena have collected cases like this, and in the last ten years over twenty-five thousand cases have been collected from all over the world.

It is important to understand that of the many people who have cardiac arrests or who are resuscitated only one out of ten has a conscious recollection of an experience during this temporary cessation of vital functioning.[1] This is very understandable if we compare it with the fact that all of us dream every night, but only a small percentage of us are aware of our dreams after we awaken.

It may be simplest to summarize what all these people experience at the moment of the cessation of physical bodily functioning. We call this simply a near death experience as all these patients have made a comeback and are able to share with us after they recovered. We will talk later about what happens to those people who do not make a comeback.

---

[1] A scientific investigation by Michael B. Sabom, *Recollections of Death*, published in 1982, shows that almost 50 percent of people who come close to death have a near-death experience.

You Cannot Die Alone

Besides an absence of pain and the experience of physical whole-ness in a simulated, perfect body, which we may call the ethereal body, people will also be aware that it is impossible to die alone. There are three reasons why no one can die alone. (And this also includes someone who dies of thirst in a desert hundreds of miles from the next human being, or an astronaut missing the target and circling around in the universe until he dies of lack of oxygen.)

Patients who are slowly preparing themselves for death, as is of-ten the case with children who have cancer, prior to death begin to be aware that they have the ability to leave their physical body and have what we call an "out-of-body" experience. All of us have these out-of-body experiences during certain states of sleep, although very few of us are consciously aware of it.

Dying children, who are much more tuned in, become much more spiritual than healthy children of the same age. They become aware of these short trips out of their body, which help them in their tran-sition, and help them to become familiar with where they are in the process of going.

It is during those out-of-body trips that dying patients become aware of the presence of beings who surround them, who guide them and help them. This is the first reason why you cannot die alone. Young children often refer to them as their playmates. The churches have called them guardian angels. Most researchers would call them guides. It is not important what label we give them. But it is important that we know that from the moment of birth, which begins with the taking of the first breath, until the moment when we make the transition and end of this physical existence, we are in the presence of these guides or guardian angels who will wait for us and help us in the transition from life to life after death.

❧

The second reason why we cannot die alone is that we will al-ways be met by those who preceded us in death and whom we have loved — a child we have lost, perhaps decades earlier, a grandmother, a father, a mother or other people who have been significant in our lives.

Californians are very frightened about this because many of them have had seven husbands and they worry which one is going to be there *(laughter from audience)*. They do not have to worry about that because after death there is no more negativity. Negativity is only a creation of man.

The third reason why we cannot die alone is that when we shed our physical bodies even temporarily prior to death, we are in an existence where there is no time and no space. And in this existence we can be anywhere we choose to be at the speed of our thought. A young man who dies in Viet Nam and thinks of his mother in Chicago will be in Chicago with the speed of his thought. If you die in the Rocky Mountains in an avalanche and your family lives in ... *(turns to audience)* where are we now? *(amusement from audience)* Virginia Beach! *(friendly laughter)* You will be in Virginia Beach at the speed of your thoughts.

Susie

A little Susie who is dying of leukemia in a hospital may be attended by her mother for weeks and weeks and it becomes very clear to the dying child that it is becoming increasingly difficult for her to leave mommy. Mommy is leaning over the aluminum side rails and implicitly or explicitly conveying to her, "Honey, don't die on me. I can't live without you." It is very hard to die that way.

So what we as parents are doing to these patients is to make them — in a sense — guilty for dying on us. This is of course very understandable.

But Susie has become more and more tuned in with total life and with the awareness of her existence after death and the full awareness of the continuation of life. During the night and during an altered state of consciousness she has been out of her body and has become aware of her ability to travel and to literally fly anywhere she wants to be. When she feels that death is imminent she will simply ask mommy to leave the hospital. She might say, "Mommy, you look so tired. Why don't you go home and take a shower, and rest a little. I'm really OK now."

The mother leaves and half an hour later a nurse may call from the hospital saying, "I'm sorry Mrs. Smith. Your daughter just passed away."

Unfortunately those parents will often live with a tremendous amount of guilt and shame, and will reprimand themselves for not having stuck it out. Just another half day and they would have been with their child at the moment of death.

What they don't know is that this didn't happen by coincidence. It is much easier for the child to let go if nobody stands there making her guilty for deserting you.

And little do the parents understand and comprehend that no one can die alone. Susie, now unburdened of her own needs, is able to let go of the cocoon and free herself quite quickly. She will then, at the speed of her thought, be with mommy or daddy or whomever she needs to be with.

❦

We all have a facet of divinity as we mentioned earlier. We received this gift seven million years ago and it includes not only the ability to have free choice but also the ability to shed our physical bodies, not only at the time of death but also in times of crisis, exhaustion, or of very extraordinary circumstances, and also in a certain kind of sleep. It is important that we know that this can also happen before death.

Victor Frankl, who wrote the very beautiful book, *The Search for Meaning,* about his experiences in the concentration camps, was probably one of the most well-known scientists who studied the out-of-body experience many decades ago when it was not yet popular. He studied people in Europe who had fallen from mountains and who, during the fall, had experienced a review of their life. He studied how many of these life experiences went through their mind during the very brief period — maybe a few seconds — of a fall from a high mountain, and he became aware that during this out-of-body experience time cannot possibly exist. Many people have had similar experiences when they have had a near drowning or during a time of their life when they were in great danger.

Our study was verified by laboratory research with the collaboration of Robert Monroe who wrote the books, *Journeys out of the Body* and *Far Journeys*. I myself have had not only spontaneous out-of-body experiences but also those that were induced in a laboratory supervised by Monroe and watched and observed and shared by several scientists from the Menninger Foundation in Topeka. More and more scientists and researchers are repeating these kinds of studies now. They have found them to be quite verifiable, and naturally they lend themselves to a great many aspects of studies of a dimension which is very hard to conceive with our three dimensional, scientific approach to life.

We have also been questioned about the guides and guardian angels, about the presence of loving human beings, especially deceased members of our family who preceded us in death, who meet us and welcome us at the time of our own transition. Again the question comes up naturally: How do you verify such frequent occurrences in a more scientific way?

Children Seeing Dead Relatives

It is interesting to me as a psychiatrist that thousands of people all around the globe should share the same hallucinations prior to death; namely, the awareness of some relatives or friends who preceded them in death. There must be some explanation for this if it's not real. And so I proceeded to try to find out means and ways to study this, to verify this. Or perhaps to verify that it is simply a projection of wishful thinking. The best way perhaps to study it is for us to sit with dying children after family accidents. We usually did this after the 4th of July, weekends, Memorial Days, Labor Days, when families go out together in family cars and all too often have head-on collisions, killing several members of the family and sending many of the injured survivors into different hospitals.

I have made it a task to sit with the critically injured children since they are my specialty. As is usually the case, they have not been told which of their family members were killed in the same accident. I was always impressed that they were invariably aware of who had preceded them in death anyway!

I sit with them, watch them silently, perhaps hold their hand, watch their restlessness and then, often shortly prior to death, a peaceful serenity comes over them. That is always an ominous sign. And that is the moment when I communicate with them. And I don't give them any ideas. I simply ask them if they are willing and able to share with me what they experience. They share in very similar words.

As one child said to me, "Everything is all right now. Mommy and Peter are already waiting for me."[2]

I was aware in this particular case that the mother had been killed immediately at the scene of the accident. But I also knew that Peter had gone to a burn unit in a different hospital and that he, as far as I knew, was still alive. I didn't give it a second thought, but as I walked out of the intensive care unit by the nursing station, I had a telephone call from the hospital where Peter was. The nurse at the other end of the line said, "Dr. Ross, we just wanted to tell you that Peter died ten minutes ago."

The only mistake I made was to say, "Yes, I know." The nurse might have thought that I was a little coo-coo.

In thirteen years of studying children near death I have never had one child who has made a single mistake when it comes to identifying — in this way — family members who have preceded them in death. I would like to see statistics on that.

The Indian Woman

There's another experience that perhaps moved me even more, and that was a case of an American Indian woman. She told me that her sister had been killed hundreds of miles away from the reservation by a hit-and-run driver. Another car stopped and the driver tried to help her. The dying woman told the stranger that he should make very, very sure to tell her mother that she was all right because she was with her father. She died after having shared that.

[2] This case report and some of the following ones are described in more detail in Elisabeth's book *On Children and Death*, chapter 13, "Spiritual Aspects of the Work with Dying Children."

The patient's father had died one hour before this accident on the reservation, seven hundred miles away from the accident scene and certainly unbeknownst to his traveling daughter.

*

One of our female patients was blinded in a laboratory explosion, and the moment she came out of her physical body she was again able to see and to describe the whole accident and the people who dashed into the laboratory. When she was brought back to life she was again totally blind. Do you understand why many, many of these people resent our attempts to artificially bring them back when they are in a far more gorgeous, more beautiful and more perfect place?

*

We also had one case of a child, a twelve-year-old child, who did not want to share with her mother that it was such a beautiful experience when she died, because no mommy likes to hear that her child has found a place that is nicer than home, and that is very understandable. But she had such a unique experience that she needed desperately to share it with somebody. One day she confided in her father. She told him that it was such a beautiful experience when she died that she did not want to come back. What made it very special, besides the whole atmosphere and the fantastic love and light that most of them convey, was that her brother was there with her, and held her with great tenderness, love and compassion. After sharing this she said to her father, "The only problem is that I don't have a brother."

Then the father confessed that she indeed did have a brother who had died, I think, three months before she was born. They had never told her of him.

Do you understand why I am bringing up examples like these? Because many people say, "Well, you know, they were not dead, and at the moment of their dying they naturally think of their loved ones, and so they naturally visualize them." But nobody could visualize a brother that she did not know of.

And we have many, many other cases like this where people who were in the process of dying have not been informed or made aware of the death of a family member, yet were greeted by them.

I ask all my terminally ill children whom they would love to see the most, whom they would love to have by their side always (meaning here and now, because many of them are nonbelieving people, whom I could not talk with about life after death. I do not impose that on my patients.) So I always ask my children, "Whom would you like to have with you always, if you could choose one person?" Ninety-nine percent of them, except for black children, say mommy or daddy. (With black children, it is very often aunties or grandmas, because those are the ones who perhaps love them the most, or have the most time with them. But those are only cultural differences.) Most of the children say mommy or daddy, but not a single one of the children who nearly died has ever seen mommy or daddy, unless their parents had preceded them in death.

Many people say, "Well, this is a projection of wishful thinking. Someone who is dying is desperate, lonely, frightened, so he imagines somebody with him whom he loves." If this were true, ninety-nine percent of all my dying children, many five-, six-, seven-year olds, would have seen their mommies or daddies.

The common denominator of who you are going to see is that he or she must have passed on before you, even if it is only one minute, and that you have genuinely loved him or her.

The Bum

There is also the case of a man who lost his entire family in a car accident in which they were all burned to death. Because of this terrible loss he turned from a money-earning, decent middle class husband and father to a total bum, who was drunk every day from morning till night and was using every conceivable drug in order to commit suicide, and yet never was able to succeed.

His last recollection was how he was lying on the edge of a forest in a dirt road, drunk and "stoned" as he called it, wanting to be reunited with his family, not wanting to live, not having the energy to even move out of the road, when he saw a big truck coming down the street and literally run over him. At this moment he watched himself in the street, critically injured, while he observed the whole scene of the accident a few feet from above, as he called it.

It was at this moment that his family appeared in front of him in a glow of light with an incredible sense of love and happy smiles on their faces, simply making him aware of their presence, not communicating in any verbal way, but in a form of a thought transference, sharing with him the joy and the happiness of their present existence.

This man was not able to tell us how long this reunion was going on, but he was so awed by their health, their beauty and radiance, by their total acceptance of his present-life situation, by their unconditional love, that he made a vow not to touch them, not to join them, but to re-enter his physical body and to promise that he would share with the world what he had experienced — in a form of a redemption for his two years of trying to throw his physical life away.

It was after this vow that he watched how the truck driver carried his injured body into the car, how an ambulance was speeding up to the scene of the accident, how he was taken to the hospital emergency room and strapped down on a stretcher. And it was in the emergency room that he finally re-entered his physical body, tore off the straps that were tied around him, and walked out of the emergency room without ever having any delirium tremens or any after effects from his heavy abuse of drugs and alcohol. He felt healed and whole and made a commitment that he would not die until he had the opportunity of sharing the existence of life after death with as many people as were willing to hear him.

We do not know what has happened to this man since then. But I will never forget the glow in his eyes, the joy and the deep gratitude he experienced when he was allowed to stand up on a stage in one of my workshops and share with a group of hundreds of hospice workers the total knowledge and awareness that our physical body is only a shell that encloses our immortal self.

Peter

The only religious differences between people from different religious backgrounds is the presence of certain religious figures. And two-year-old Peter is perhaps our best example. He had an anaphylactic allergic reaction to a drug given to him by a physician in a doctor's office and was declared dead. While the physician and the mother waited for the father to arrive, the mother desperately touched her little boy, cried and sobbed and pleaded with him. After what seemed to her an eternity, her little two-year old opened his eyes and said in a voice of an old, wise man, "Mommy, I was dead. I was in the most beautiful place and I didn't want to come back. I was with Jesus and Mary."

Mary kept telling him that the time was not right, so he had to go back. He tried to ignore her, which is very typical of two-year-olds, and as he tried to do that, Mary apparently took him gently by his wrist and pulled him away saying, "Peter, you *have* to go back. You will have to save your mother from the fire."

It was at this moment that Peter opened his eyes, and he said with a happy voice, "You know mommy, when she told me that I ran all the way back home."

The mother was not able to share this incident for thirteen years and was rather depressed because of her misinterpretation of Mary's statement to Peter. Her misunderstanding was that her son meant he was eventually the one who had to save her from the fire of Hell. And she couldn't understand why she was supposed to be doomed to Hell as she was a very decent, hardworking woman of faith.

I tried to convey to her that she had not understood the symbolic language, and that this was a unique and beautiful gift of Mary who, like all beings in the spiritual realm, is a being of total and unconditional love, unable to condemn or to criticize, which are qualities that only human beings have. I asked her for a moment to stop thinking and to simply allow her own spiritual intuitive quadrant to respond. And then I asked her, "What would it have been like if Mary hadn't sent Peter back to you thirteen years ago?" She grabbed her hair and shouted, "Oh my God, I would have gone through hell and fire."

It was no longer necessary for me to say, "Now, do you understand that Mary saved you from the fire?"

Corry

This is one of my favorite dying patients, a five-year-old boy from Seattle. He has been slowly dying and that is not easy. He is now expected to live maybe for another week. From time to time he calls me up when he has a question or some unfinished business.

In the last few months he has had occasional near-death experiences. He is very old and very wise and only five years old. He is not afraid to die. He tells all the children in the hospital what it's like to die in minute details.

The last near-death experience he sent me was this picture and I don't know if you can see it down there (holds picture for audience to see).

In the left upper quadrant, which always reveals the concept of death, is a very colorful castle. When he came back, he said to his mother, "This is God, this is his castle with a smiling, dancing star." The star told him, "Welcome back home, Corry!" That was his experience.

Then he asked me to show all of you this picture, because you see there is a rainbow. He said, "This is not only a rainbow, it is really the side view of the bridge that goes from this life into the next life." So I told you and I kept my promise, right?

And after he had had this near death experience, he was worried again for a moment and he called me up again and said that he really needed to know whether his dog, Quasar, was going to be there waiting for him. Quasar had died two weeks earlier.

You don't learn in medical school how to answer that kind of question. So I said to him, "You know, all I know is that we may not always get what we want, but we are always given what we really need. So if you really need it, all you have to do is ask and then maybe Quasar will be there waiting for you."

Then, after his next near-death experience, he called up very excited and said, "Elisabeth, Elisabeth! Not only was Quasar there, but he even wiggled his tail!"

The Tunnel and the Light

The Scriptures are full of symbolic language and if people would listen more to their intuitive, spiritual quadrant and not contaminate the understanding of these beautiful messages with their own negativity, their own fears, their own guilt, and their own needs to punish others or themselves, they would begin to comprehend the beautiful symbolic language that dying patients use when they try to convey their needs to us, their knowledge and their awareness.

Needless to say it would be unlikely for a Jewish child to see Jesus. A Protestant child would probably not see Mary. Not that they would not care for those children, but simply because we always get what we need the most. The ones we meet are the ones we have loved the most and who preceded us in death.

After we are met by those we have loved, and by our own guides and guardian angels, we are passing through a symbolic transition often described in the form of a tunnel, a river, a gate. Each one will choose what is most symbolically appropriate for him. In my own personal experience it was naturally a mountain pass with wild flowers simply because my concept of Heaven includes mountains and wild flowers, the source of much happiness in my childhood in Switzerland. This is culturally determined.

After we pass through this visually very beautiful and individually appropriate form of transition, called the tunnel, we approach a source of light that many of our patients describe and that I have myself experienced in the form of an incredibly beautiful and unforgettable life-changing experience called "Cosmic Consciousness."

In the presence of this light, which most people in our western hemisphere call "Christ" or "God" or "Love" or "Light," we are surrounded by total and absolute, unconditional love, understanding and compassion. We are in the presence of this light, which is a source of pure spiritual energy and no longer physical or psychic energy. Spiritual energy can neither be manipulated nor used by human beings. It is an energy in the realm of existence where negativity is impossible. And that means that no matter how bad we have been in our life or how guilty we feel, we are unable to experience any negative emotions. It is also totally impossible to be condemned in this presence, which many people call "Christ" or "God," since he is a being of total and absolute unconditional love.

The Life Review

In this presence we become aware of our potential — of what we *could* be like, of what we *could* have lived like. It is also in this presence, surrounded by compassion, love and understanding, that we are asked to review and evaluate our total existence. Since we are no longer attached to a mind or physical brain and a limiting physical body, we have all knowledge and all understanding. It is in this existence that we have to review and evaluate every thought, every word and every deed of our existence. And we will be simultaneously aware of how all of this has affected others.

In the presence of this spiritual energy we no longer have the need for a physical form. And we then leave this ethereal, simulated body behind and resume again the form that we had before we were born and the form we will have in eternity between lifetimes, and the form we will have when we merge with the Source, with God, when we have finished our destiny.

It is important to understand that from the moment of the beginning of our existence until we return to God we always maintain our own identity and our own energy pattern. That means that among the billions of people in this universe on this physical plane and in the unobstructed world there are no two energy patterns, no two people alike, not even identical twins.

If anybody doubts the greatness of our Creator one should consider what genius it takes to create billions of energy patterns and no two alike. This is the uniqueness of the human being. And the only thing I could compare this miracle with is the number of snowflakes on the planet Earth.

I have had the great blessing of being able to see with my own physical eyes the presence of hundreds of those energy patterns in full daylight. And it is very similar to a fluttering, pulsating series of different snowflakes, all with their different lights and colors and their different forms and shapes. This is what we look like after we die. This is also how we exist before we are born. We take up no space, and it takes no time for us to go from one star to another or from planet Earth to another galaxy. And those energy patterns, those beings, are with us right here, and if we only had the eyes to see them we would be aware that we are never ever alone. We are surrounded by these beings who guide us, who love us, who protect us, who try to direct us to help us to go on the track where we have to be to fulfill our own destiny.

Maybe in times of great pain, of great sorrow, or of great loneliness, we can get tuned in and become aware of their presence. We can communicate with them at night before we fall asleep and we can ask them to make their presence known to us. We can ask them questions before we fall asleep and ask them to give us an answer in our dreams. Those who have been tuned in to their sleep states, to their dreams, become aware that many of our questions are answered in this state. And as we get more tuned in to our own *inner* entity, to our own inner spiritual part, it is very understandable that we can get help and guidance also from our *o w n* inner entity, from our own all-knowing self, that immortal part we call the butterfly.

Mrs. Schwartz's Visit

I have not finished telling you the story of Mrs. Schwartz and I am going to run out of time, I am sure. I want to add that she died two weeks after her son came of age. She was buried, and she was one of many patients of mine, and I am sure I would have forgotten her if she had not visited me again. Approximately ten months after she was dead and buried, I was in troubles. I am always in troubles, but at that time I was in bigger troubles than usual. My seminar on death and dying had started to deteriorate. The minister with whom I had worked and whom I loved very dearly had left. The new minister was very conscious of publicity, and the course became accredited.

Every week we had to talk about the same stuff, and it was like the famous date show. It was not worth it. It was like prolonging life when it is no longer worth living. It was something that was not me, and I decided that the only way that I could stop it was to physically leave the University of Chicago. Naturally my heart broke, because I really loved this work, but not that way. So I made a heroic decision. I told myself, "I am going to leave the University of

Chicago, and today, immediately after my death and dying seminar, I am going to give notice."

The minister and I had a ritual. After the seminar we would go to the elevator, I would wait for his elevator to come, we would finish business talk, he would leave, and I would go back to my office, which was on the same floor at the end of a long hallway.

The minister's biggest problem was that he could not hear — this was another of my grievances. And so, between the classroom and the elevator, I tried three times to tell him that it was all his, that I was leaving. He didn't hear me. He kept talking about something else. I got very desperate, and when I am desperate I become very active. Before the elevator arrived — he was a huge guy — I finally grabbed his collar, and I said, "You're gonna stay right here. I have made a horribly important decision, and I want you to know what it is."

I really felt like a hero to be able to do that. He didn't say anything.

At this moment a woman appeared in front of the elevator. I stared at her. I cannot tell you how this woman looked, but you can imagine what it is like when you see somebody that you know terribly well, but you suddenly block out who it is. I said to him, "God, who is this? I know this woman, and she is staring at me; she is just waiting until you go into the elevator, and then she will come."

I was so preoccupied with who she was that I forgot that I was trying to grab him. She stopped that. She was very transparent, but not transparent enough that you could see very much behind her. I asked him once more, and he didn't tell me who it was, so I gave up on him. The last thing I said to him was kind of, "Heck, I'm going over and tell her I just cannot remember her name." That was my last thought before he left.

The moment he entered the elevator, the woman walked straight toward me and said, "Dr. Ross, I had to come back. Do you mind if I walk you to your office? It will only take two minutes." Something like this. And because she knew where my office was, and she knew my name, I was kind of safe, I didn't have to admit that I didn't know who she was.

This was the longest path I have ever walked in my whole life. I am a psychiatrist. I work with schizophrenic patients all the time, and I love them. When they were having visual hallucinations I told them a thousand times, "I know you see that Madonna on the wall, but I don't see it." I said to myself, "Elisabeth, I know you see this woman, but that can't be."

Do you understand what I'm doing? All the way from the elevator to my office I did reality testing on myself. I said, "I'm tired, I need a vacation. I think I have seen too many schizophrenic patients. I'm beginning to see things. I have to touch her, to see if she is real." I even touched her skin to see if it was cold or warm, or if the skin would disappear when I touched it. It was the most incredible walk I have ever taken, but not knowing all the way why I was doing what I was doing. I was both an observing psychiatrist and a patient. I was both at the same time. I didn't know why I did what I did, or who I thought she was. I even repressed the thought that this could actually be Mrs. Schwartz who had died and had been buried months ago.

When we reached my door, she opened it like I was a guest in my own house. She opened it with such an incredible kindness and tenderness and love, and she said, "Dr. Ross, I had to come back for two reasons. One is to thank you and Reverend Gaines." (He was that beautiful black minister with whom I had had this super-ideal symbiosis). "To thank you and him for what you did for me. But the real reason I had to come back is that you cannot stop your work on death and dying, not yet."

I looked at her, and I don't know if I thought by then that this could be Mrs. Schwartz. I mean, this woman had been buried for ten months and I didn't believe in all that stuff. I finally got to my desk. I touched my pen, my desk and my chair, which was all real, you know, hoping that she would disappear. But she didn't disappear; she just stood there and stubbornly but lovingly said, "Dr. Ross, do you hear me? Your work is not finished. We will help you, and you will know when the time is right, but do not stop now, promise."

I thought, "My God, nobody would ever believe me if I told them about this, not even my dearest friend." Little did I know then that

I would say this to several hundred people. Then the scientist in me won, and I said to her something that was very shrewd and a real big, fat lie. I said, "You know, Reverend Gaines is in Urbana now."

So far it was true; he had taken over a church there. But then I said, "He would just love to have a note from you. Would you mind?"

And I gave her a piece of paper and a pencil. You understand, I had no intention of sending this note to my friend, but I needed scientific proof. I mean, somebody who is buried can't write little love letters. And this woman, with the most human — no, not human — most loving smile, knowing every thought I had — and I knew, it was thought transference if I've ever experienced it — took this paper and wrote this note, which we naturally have framed in glass and treasure dearly. Then she said, but without words, she said, "Are you satisfied now?"

I looked at her and thought, "I will never be able to share this with anybody, but I am going to really hold on to this. Then she got up, ready to leave, repeating, "Dr. Ross, you promise," implying not to give up this work yet. I said, "I promise." And the moment I said, "I promise," she left.

We still have her note.

One of My First Mystical Experiences

Let me share with you now some of my own mystical experiences that helped me truly know rather than believe that all these existences beyond the realm of our scientific understanding are true, are reality, are something that is available to all human beings. I have to make it very clear that in my earlier years I had no comprehension of higher consciousness. I never had a guru. In fact I was never really able to meditate, which is a source of great peace and understanding for many people, not only in the eastern hemisphere but in more and more of the western world too. On the other hand it is true that I am getting totally tuned in when I communicate with dying patients. And maybe those thousands of hours that I have been sitting with them where nothing and no one was able to distract us may be considered a form of meditation. If that is true, then I have indeed meditated for many, many hours.

But I truly believe that it is not important to go to a mountain top, to live as a hermit, to go to India or to have a guru in order to have these mystical experiences. I truly believe that every human being consists of a physical, an emotional, an intellectual and a spiritual quadrant. And if we can learn to externalize our unnatural feelings and emotions, our hate and anguish, our unresolved grief and our oceans of unshed tears, then we can get back to and into what we usually were meant to be. And that is a human being, consisting of four quadrants, all of which work together in total harmony and wholeness.

These four quadrants can work together in harmony only if we accept and love our physicalness, only if we are able to share our natural emotions without being handicapped by them, only if we are able to express natural anger, only if we are able to feel the natural jealousy which helps us emulate someone else's talents, only if we are able to understand that we have only two natural fears, one of falling and one of loud noises, and that all the other fears have been given to us by grownups who projected their own fears onto us, thus passing them on from generation to generation.

And most important of all, these four quadrants can work together in harmony if we have learned to love and be loved unconditionally.

Most of us have been raised as prostitutes, "I love you *if...*" And this word "if" has ruined and destroyed more lives than anything else on this planet Earth. It prostitutes us, it makes us feel that we can buy love with good behavior or good grades and it stops us from developing a sense of self-love and self-worth.

Also, the four quadrants can work in harmony only if we have been taught by consistent, loving discipline instead of by punishment. The spiritual teachers taught us: If you have been raised with unconditional love and discipline you will never be afraid of the windstorms of life. You will have no fear, no guilt and no anxieties — the only enemies of man.

Should you shield the canyons from the windstorms, you would never see the beauty of their carvings.

And so I went about, not looking for a guru, not trying to meditate, not trying to reach a higher state of consciousness. But each time a patient or a life situation made me aware of some negativity within me, I tried to externalize it so I would eventually reach that harmony between my physical, emotional, spiritual and intellectual quadrant. And as I did my homework and tried to practice, I would go around teaching. I was blessed with more and more mystical experiences, which means getting in touch with my own intuitive, spiritual, all-knowing and all-understanding self. But I was also able to get in touch with the guidance which comes from the unobstructed world, and which always surrounds us and waits for an occasion, an opportunity to not only impinge on us with knowledge and direction, but also to help us to understand what life and especially our own personal destiny is all about, so that we might fulfill our destiny in one lifetime and not have to return in order to learn the lessons we have not been able to pass in this existence.

***

One of my first experiences was during a research project where I was allowed to experience out-of-body experiences induced by iatrogenic means in a laboratory in Virginia, observed and attended by several skeptical scientists.

I was lying on a water bed in a kind of booth. After a short while I was hovering under the ceiling. I wanted to see how the ceiling was built, because it is possible to penetrate all kinds of matter. It was very exciting. But I was slowed down and called back by the laboratory chief who felt that I went too fast too soon. Much to my dismay, he in a way interfered with my own needs and my own personality.

To Say Yes to It

The next time I was in the booth I felt that I couldn't trust the laboratory chief. He was too careful, so I was determined to circumvent this problem by giving myself a self-induction to go faster than the speed of light and further than any human being had ever gone in an out-of-body experience. The moment the induction was given I literally left my body at an incredible speed. Suddenly I realized that I was going horizontally and that was the wrong direction, and so I turned ninety degrees and went away vertically. It was very exciting! I went as fast as I could and as far away as I could so that no one would catch up with me. I felt very secure. No one would be able to find me. I was literally in a place where nobody had been before, and after that I have no memory of what happened to me.

The only memory I had when I returned to my physical body was the words *Shanti Nilaya*. I had no idea of the meaning or significance of these words, and had no concept of where I had been. The only awareness I had was that I was healed of an almost complete bowel obstruction and also of a very painful slipped disk which had made it impossible for me even to pick up a book from the floor.

When I came out of this experiment my bowel obstruction was healed and I was able to lift a hundred pound sugar bag from the floor without any discomfort or pain. I was told that I radiated, that I looked twenty years younger, and everybody present tried to press me for information. I had no idea where I had been until the night after the experiment, a night I spent in a lonely guest house alone in a forest in the Blue Ridge Mountains when gradually and not without trepidation the awareness came to me that I had gone too far and that I had now to accept the consequences of my own choices.

I tried to fight sleep that night, having a vague and inner knowledge that *it* would happen, not knowing what *it* would mean.

And the moment I let go I had probably the most painful, most agonizing experience any human being can ever live through. I literally lived through the thousand deaths of the thousand patients that I had attended up till that time. I lived through all the blood, all the pain, the incredible agony and tears and isolation — every negative aspect of every patient's death. And this repeated itself a thousand times — every time a different way, but still the same pains.

It was a total physical, spiritual, emotional and intellectual agony with inability to breathe, with a doubling up of my body in agonizing physical pain and a total knowledge and awareness that I was out of reach of any human being and that I had to make it somehow through that night.

In these agonizing hours I had only three reprieves. It was very similar to going through labor pains and after each labor pain, another one follows immediately without an instant to breathe in between. In those three brief moments when I was able to catch a breath, some significant symbolic occurrences happened which I understood only much later on. During the first reprieve I begged for a shoulder to lean on. And I expected a man's left shoulder to appear, so I could put my head on it and bear the agony somewhat better. In the same instant that I asked for the shoulder to lean on, a deep, caring, compassionate and severe voice simply stated, "You shall not be given."

An endless amount of time later I had another moment to catch a breath. And this time I begged for a hand to hold. And again I expected a hand to show up at the right side of my bed so I could grab on to it and endure the agony somewhat easier. And the same voice appeared again, "You shall not be given."

The third and the last time I was able to catch a breath I contemplated asking for a finger tip. Naturally you cannot hold onto a finger tip but at least it gives you the awareness of the presence of a human being. And very much in character with myself I said, "No. If I can't get a single hand I don't want a finger tip either." That was my conclusion. Even I deserve an absolute minimum, and *my* absolute minimum is a hand. A finger tip is not enough.

Then I went through more pain and agony, and I thought, "I have been holding the hand of so many patients who have been lonely and desperate and dying. Why can't I have a hand to hold on to? Am I so bad? Am I a bad human being?"

Then, for the first time in my life it became an issue of faith. And the faith had something to do with a deep inner knowledge that I had the strength and the courage to endure this agony all by myself. But it also included the faith and the knowledge that we are never given more than we can bear.

I suddenly became aware that all I needed to do was to stop my fight, to stop my rebellion, to stop being a warrior and to move from rebellion to a simple, peaceful, positive submission, to an ability to simply say yes to it.

And the moment I did that the agony stopped. My breathing was easier, my physical pain disappeared, with the moment I uttered the word *Yes*, not in words but in thoughts.

And instead of the thousand deaths, I lived through a rebirth experience which is beyond any human description.

It started with a very fast vibration or pulsation of my abdominal wall, which spread throughout my entire body and then spread onto anything that my eyes touched. I looked down on my abdominal wall and what I saw was not anatomically possible. (I observed this scientifically while I was living through it. It was as if I had a second, observing me watching what was going on.)

Whatever I looked at started to vibrate: the ceiling, the wall, the floors, the furniture, the bed, the window, the horizons outside of my window, the trees — and eventually the vibrations included the whole planet Earth. It was as if the whole planet Earth was in a very high, speedy vibration. Every molecule vibrated, and at the same time in front of me appeared something that looked like a lotus flower bud, which opened into an incredibly beautiful, colorful flower. And behind the lotus flower appeared the light that my patients so often had talked about. And as I approached this light through the open lotus flower with the world in a deep, fast vibration, I gradually and slowly merged into this incredible, unconditional love, into this light. And I became one with it.

At the moment of the merging into this source of light all vibrations stopped. A deep silence came over me and I fell into a deep, trance-like sleep from which I awoke knowing that I had, in awhile, I would have to wear a robe and put my sandals on, and walk down the hill, and that this would occur at the moment when the sun rose from behind the horizon.

Approximately an hour and a half later I woke up, put the robe on, wore my sandals and walked down the hill and experienced probably the greatest ecstasy of existence that human beings can ever experience on this physical plane. I was in total love and awe of all life around me. I was in love with every leaf, every cloud, every grass, every little creature. I felt the pulsation of the pebbles on the path and I literally walked above the pebbles, conveying to them, "I cannot step on you. I cannot hurt you."

As I reached the bottom of the hill I became aware that I had not touched the ground on this path but there was no questioning about the validity of the experience. Simply an awareness of a cosmic consciousness of life in every living thing and of a love that can never, ever be described in words.

<hr />

It took me several days to come back to physical existence with its trivialities of washing dishes, doing the laundry, and cooking meals for my family.

It took several months before I was able to verbalize my experience. I shared it with a beautiful, nonjudgmental, understanding group who invited me to speak at a conference on transpersonal psychology in Berkeley, California.

Cosmic Consciousness

After I shared my experience I was given a label for it. It was called "Cosmic Consciousness." And as usual I had to go to the library, find a book with the same title to learn intellectually and to comprehend the meaning of such a state.

I was also told at that moment that the word that was given to me as I merged into this spiritual energy, the source of all light — *Shanti Nilaya* — is Sanskrit and it means *The Final Home of Peace*, the home that all of us will return to when we have gone through all the agonies, the pain, the sorrows, the grief, and when we are able to let go of the pain and become what we were created to be: a being of harmony between the physical, the emotional, the intellectual, and the spiritual quadrants, a being that understands that love, true love, has no claims and no "ifs," and that if we can understand this state of love, then all of us will be whole and healthy and all of us will be able to fulfill our destiny in one single lifetime.

This experience has touched and changed my life in ways that are very difficult to put into words. But I think that it was because of this experience that I also understood that if I ever wished to share my understanding of life after death, I would literally have to go through a thousand deaths, that the society in which I live would try to shred me to pieces, and that the experience — the knowledge, the joy, the love and the sensation of what followed the agony, the rewards would always be far greater than the pain. It is this single experience during that night in the Blue Ridge Mountains that made it possible for me to continue to lecture, to continue to do our research in spite of all the negative publicity, and in spite of all the people who have to project their own negativity onto us, because it is unacceptable to them to take responsibility for their own life and their own negativities.

It is only because of this understanding and the knowledge that it will all be worth it, that we were given probably the greatest experience of a lifetime. And that is to experience what our patients experience at the moment of death, to be allowed to experience the physical presence of our own guides without having to go out through permanent death.

In the mid 1970s, I was invited to a group that was informed by me that it would be the day that Elisabeth K. Ross would meet with her own guides, but that I would not believe this miracle if it were not witnessed by seventy-five people, that I would not believe it if I could not tape record it, that I would not believe it if all the people present did not see it with their own eyes.

It was during that night that, in a darkened room, witnessed and tape-recorded by seventy-five people from all walks of life, from different professions and different backgrounds, that I was given another experience of what most of you will only experience at the moment of death.

Within a few minutes a large figure, seven foot ten, appeared in front of me and started to talk with me. And a few moments later my own friend by the name of Salem appeared in front of me and not only touched my sandals but also stroked my hair and held my hand. And I experienced the unconditional love, the compassion and understanding that we only normally comprehend at the time when we leave our physical body.

It was at that time that we were told what this work was all about and that we should go out into the world and share that all of you have this guidance, all of you are loved beyond comprehension, all of you are blessed and guided, if you are only honest and willing enough to look the Hitler within you, externalize it, and try to learn unconditional love, compassion instead of judgment, empathy instead of pity, and realize that this life in a physical body is a very short span of your total existence. It is a school where we choose our own minor and major, where we choose our own teachers, where all of us have to go through tests, trials and tribulations. And when we have passed the tests, we are allowed to graduate and return back home where we all came from and where we all will be reunited again one day.

Thank you for listening to me.

Elisabeth Kübler-Ross on farm (Eva's house)

Elisabeth Kübler-Ross on farm

Healing in Our Time

(*Elisabeth is not the first one to give her speech at this seminar. A man introduces her somewhat solemnly, "We thank the beautiful people who have organized this seminar for bringing into our midst ... one of the loveliest, most distinguished women of our age. This woman has received much love. This woman has given much love. Elisabeth Kübler-Ross, you are a celebrator of life, and you honor us with your presence. Thank you!") (Applause)*

(*Elisabeth starts a little hesitantly:*) Thank you ... Thank you ... Thank you ... It's very touching ... to see so many people ... and to see how people are ready... for a lot of new things to come. I don't know how many of you followed what was said since eight o'clock ... I didn't! (*surprised laughter from audience*)

But that is how it should be! I'm not saying that with any negative connotation. We are in such an exciting time where so many new things are coming up that I don't think any single individual person understands what Olga is doing, what Selma is doing, what Elmer is doing — what I am doing.

Many people who don't understand what we are doing say that we are crazy, and that we are psychotic, or that we have lost our reality testing, or also they give us some very funny labels. And if you get those labels, regard it as a blessing (*surprised silence and then warm laughter and applause*) regard it as a blessing. I am naturally psychotic (*laughter*) all the time — if you define reality testing in a very limited manner, in only understanding the things that happen to all people and are understood by all people.

There is a beautiful poster in my office that says, "To avoid criticism: say nothing, do nothing, be nothing." That is one choice that people have. You people who are in this audience do not belong to that group. But that does not make you superior — I hope you hear that also. Because a child who goes to high school would not knock a brother or a sister who is in kindergarten.

We are beginning to see that life in its physical form is literally nothing but a school where we learn, where we grow, where we have to pass a lot of tests. And the higher up we get in the evolution, the tougher the tests. Then we will also begin to understand that nobody is a teacher, that nobody is a student; we have just students at different levels.

Why do I say all this? When I listen to statements [from a previous lecture] like, "the normal brain limits our awareness" all I can write down is, "Thank God!" *(surprised silence from audience)* And I think it gives me even more of a sense of awe about God, how well He knew man, that He created a brain that limits us. Because if the brain didn't have any limitations, then we could never take it, we could not tolerate it. It is as if man suddenly were able to have an orgasm for twenty-four hours: who would wash the dishes! *(big laughter and applause)* I don't even mean that jokingly! *(more laughter)*

It is to me a gift to be a human being, and the little children that are born now — I was visited by a three-week-old baby in my room before coming down — I look at those babies and I say, "What a miracle!" I mean, here in Washington are all these brains together: how many of you could recreate something like this baby even if you had a hundred-billion dollars? Nobody could re-create it. Nobody.

I'm spending my life with no theories about higher consciousness, but with the healing of human beings very much on the ground. And yet if I had not been on the other side, I would not be able to do what I'm doing. I would never be able to be with dying children, with parents of murdered children, with the mother who stepped out to get the bottle of milk and came back to find her three sons shot in the neck, with a couple who lost all their children from cancer within six months, with a young physician who watched his father die of Huntington's disease at age forty becoming senile, watched him for years and years and years wondering, "Am I one of the fifty percent in the family who will get it also?" then beginning to develop symptoms and looking at his preschool children, knowing that in three years he too would be like his father was a few years before his death. And the only solution this man can think of is suicide.

I could never work eighteen hours a day, seven days a week, seeing anguish, agony and pain and horror if I could not see the other side of the coin also. And if people began to learn the meaning of life, and the meaning even of the pain, and the meaning even of the tragedies, and the incredible miracle of human life, then they would bless it every day, not only the joys and the heights but, especially, perhaps the difficult periods of time.

The Paralyzed Woman

I received a phone call some time ago from a young nurse, who, out of loving care, had promised her mother to take her home to die if she should ever become anything close to a vegetable, or if she should become dependent on machines, because in their definition this would not be living. They promised each other to totally and fully live and love as long as they were in their physical bodies. I asked her why she called and she said, "All I wanted to ask is one little favor, and that is that you talk to my mother, because today is the last day that she can speak."

Her mother had a rapidly progressing neurological disease and they could see how the paralysis progressed from day to day from her toes on up, and they knew almost to the day when she would no longer be able to speak, then no longer be able to breathe. By then, she would have to choose to exist on a respirator or actually die. This was the last day that she would be able to speak.

I thought that that was a very simple request so I said, "sure, put the telephone on your mother's ear." She put it on her ear, and the mother tried to speak, and I absolutely did not understand what she tried to say. If you live with people it is easier, but over the telephone it was totally impossible. It is very important that we are honest, that we do not pretend that we understand children or patients when we don't.

So I told the daughter, "I don't know what she is talking about, but she has some very important unfinished business that she needs to share. Unfortunately I'm leaving for Europe." And I asked her impulsively, "How far away do you live?" She said, "Four hours from where you are." I said, "That's too bad. If it were three hours, I could make it back and forth in six. Eight hours is impossible. I have to catch a plane." And then, impulsive as I am, I said, "But I do believe in miracles. If I need to see your mother I'll be able to see her. One possibility is that you put her in a van" (she was paralyzed up to her neck) "and you hit the road towards where I live and I come from the other way and we will make a 'street corner consultation'." *(laughter)* I don't know a better name for it, but I do that all the time. As long as you know your geography, it works.

And this young daughter, who happened to be a nurse said, "I believe in miracles too. My mother's house is on the other side of Los Angeles and if I bring her there, you can make it in time and still catch your plane for Switzerland."

All I needed to do was to find a friend who was not afraid of cops *(laughter)* and who could really, you know, speed to Los Angeles. We hopped into a car, we were almost flying to L.A.

I walked into this woman's house. And you know how we project our own expectations. I expected a fifty-five year old woman, which was my age at that time, to be in bed, paralyzed up to the neck, depressed, miserable and unhappy. And when I walked in I saw that she had the biggest beaming smile all over her face.

I tried to talk to her and to figure out what she was trying to tell me. This is what she was saying: She wanted to thank me for making it possible for her to die at home. She had been taken home by her daughter and if she had not been at one of my lectures, she would have been on a respirator now, and that would not have been such a horrible nightmare, though very unpleasant. But then she would have been cheated out of the greatest gift of her life which was the presence of her new grandchild, who was born twelve weeks earlier. She said, "We would never have been able to see each other. Because we still have those signs in the hospital: 'No children allowed'."

She wanted to thank me. I said, "Tell me what it was like, so I can pass it on, what it was like that night when you knew that the next morning you would no longer be able to move your arms and your fingers. What was it like? A few months ago you could walk around in the garden, take care of everything. "And now she was literally dead up to her neck.

And again instead of making a long, sad, tragic face, drowning herself in very understandable self-pity, she had an even bigger smile and she said (all her communications were with the help of a speaking board!), "I have to tell you what happened. Because the morning I woke up and my arms were paralyzed, then everything was paralyzed up to my chin. My daughter realized the situation and walked into my room and very quietly put this three-month-old baby in my paralyzed arms. And I simply watched her. Suddenly this little girl lifted up her fingers and her hands and her arms and discovered them. I said to myself: 'What an incredible blessing. I had it for fifty-five years, and now I can pass it on to my granddaughter.'"

Then she started to drool, and since I am an old meany I said, "drooling like this! Brrr!" I said, "I'm sure a few months ago you would not have liked having visitors watching you drool like this all over the place." And she laughed and said, "You are damned right. A few months ago I wouldn't want anybody to see me this way. But you know what? Now the two of us drool together and laugh together." *(laughter from audience)*

In a very brief nutshell, this is what I'm trying to share with you: you do not appreciate the gifts you have. Very few of you appreciate that you can go to the bathroom, that you can walk, that you can dance, that you can sing, that you can laugh. You have to wait until you lose it, and then you bless what you had in a past tense.

If you reached higher consciousness, can you imagine how tragic it would be? Because you would not appreciate what you have unless it happens for a few glimpses of a moment just to give you a taste of what you could have all the time once you appreciate what you already have. Does that make sense?

It is very simple. Anybody and everybody can heal. Anybody and everybody can have every degree of higher consciousness. And you do not need to do anything about it, except appreciate what you have and get rid of the things that block you from fully appreciating what you have. And I will tell you in very plain, practical language how to do that.

Do not look for gurus or babas. The teachers you will get in your life are the most unlikely people in the world. In the years that I started my work on death and dying at the University of Chicago I was very much a *persona non grata*. People would spit at me and humiliate me in public because I was a physician who tried to work with dying patients. It was very difficult and very painful and very lonely and very hard *(with the slightest pain in her voice)*. They called me the v.. vul.. vulture. It seems like a hundred years ago.

When you are very alone, very isolated, and you walk on very thin ice, you have to be very careful, you will have to know exactly how far you can go before the ice breaks. It is literally a question of be or not to be. If you go too fast too soon you lose everything you have gained. This is also true when you try to share with other people about experiences of higher consciousness. If you are not sure, go slow. And if you are still not sure, then keep quiet. Because it just means that those who are listening to you are not yet ready for it. And that is OK!

It was very difficult. I had nobody to support me. I was in a very difficult, precarious life situation and it was only the patients who supported me. They gave me the message: you are at the right place, continue to do it. Every patient would kind of sustain me to the next one, and then to the next one. During that very vulnerable time I became a very good psychiatrist because I was hyperalert as to whom to trust and whom to go very slowly with.

In those days, when I was very alone, I really needed moral support. The hospital chaplains had not yet associated and I was there alone except for one woman, a black cleaning woman.

The Black Cleaning Woman*

That black cleaning woman was my greatest teacher. I will have to give her credit for what I have learned as long as I live. *She* is the one to get credit for it. And she doesn't know how much she did.

---

* Since my stroke, I can no longer recall the name of this woman or of many other people who have been important to me.

This black cleaning woman in the university hospital had a gift that was totally beyond my comprehension. She was totally uneducated and had never been to high school and certainly had no academic understanding. But there was something about her, and I didn't know what it was. I was dying to know what in the world she did with my dying patients. Every time she walked into the room of one of my dying patients something happened in that room. And I would have given a million dollars to learn that woman's secret.

One day I saw her in the hallway. I said to myself, "You always tell your medical students: if you have a question, for Heaven's sake ask," and I gave myself a big push and quickly approached her. I said to her, rather curtly, "What are you doing with my dying patients?" *(laughter from audience)*

Of course she became paranoid and very defensive, and she said, "I'm not doing anything, I'm only cleaning the room." *(amusement from audience)* I came from Switzerland, so I couldn't understand that a black cleaning woman would have a problem talking to a white professor of psychiatry.

I said to her, "That's not what I'm talking about." But she didn't trust me and walked away.

❦

We snooped around each other for weeks *(laughter)*. You know what snooping around means? This is the simplest example of symbolic nonverbal language. That is what people do who try to get to know each other, who try to find out who you really are, not what you wear or your external form.

After weeks of snooping around like this, she had the courage to just grab me and drag me into a back room behind the nursing station. There she opened her heart and her soul to me and told me a very dramatic story, which to me was totally disconnected with my question and was totally beyond *my* intellectual comprehension. I had no idea at that time what was going on.

She told me how she grew up on 63rd Street in a very bad, bad, poor neighborhood. No food, very sick children, no medicines. On one occasion she sat in the county hospital with her three-year-old boy on her lap, desperately waiting hours for a physician to come, and watching her little boy die of pneumonia in her arms.

And the issue about this woman was that she shared all this pain and agony without hate, without resentment, without anger, and without negativity. In those days I was very naive, and I was just ready to say to her, "Why are you telling me all this? What has this to do with my dying patients?" And as if she could read my mind she said, "You see, Dr. Ross, death is not a stranger to me anymore. He is like an old, old acquaintance. I am not afraid of him anymore. Sometimes when I walk into the room of your dying patients, they look so scared. I can't help but walk over to them and touch them and say, 'It's not so terrible.'"

<hr>

If it had not been for this woman — and I mean that from the bottom of my heart in the most concrete way — if it had not been for that woman, I do not think I would have lasted. This is what I'm trying to say: do not look for gurus or babas. Your teachers come disguised. They come in the form of children, they come in the form of senile, old grandmas, and they come in the form of a black cleaning woman.

This woman does not know who she is. And she does not know what role she played and how many lives she has touched as a consequence of her choices. It does not matter *what* you do in life. The only thing that matters is that you do what you do with love.

I promoted this woman to my first assistant much to the dismay of my academic colleagues *(laughter and applause)*. Because what this woman... *(Elisabeth interrupts herself, turns to audience and very gently says:)* If you are honest: how many of you applauded out of hostility? *(surprised silence from audience)*

How many of you applauded with hostility? *(continued silence fro m audience)*

Hostility *against* the physicians and the establishment? *(scattere d applause and laughter and finally a "Bravo!")* Yes! As long as you do that, you are responsible for things not being better *(reluctant, scattered applause). (still very gently)* It is very important that you learn that. We curse, we question, we judge and we criticize, and any time we judge or criticize, we add negativity to the world.

Ask yourself why a high school kid should knock a first grader. Do you understand what I said before? It is only arrogance that makes people do that. Do I make myself clear? *(reluctant applause)*

(Very gently): If you want to *heal* the world it is terribly important to understand that *you cannot heal the world without first healing thyself.* As long as you knock and judge and criticize anybody, *you* are responsible for a Hiroshima, Nagasaki, Viet Nam, Maidaneck or an Auschwitz. And I mean that literally *(silence from audience).*

In my Death and Dying seminars, to digress for a minute, we included randomly selected dying patients. I was a novice, and I depended on my patients to be the teachers and God forbid I was ever to be stuck ten minutes without a patient. I wouldn't have known what to say: That was ten thousand years ago *(laughter).* Actually only thirteen years ago.

One day my patient died ten minutes before the seminar and I had a two-hour class with nothing to talk about. And I was a novice, I mean a total novice. All the way to my classroom I was talking to everybody saying, "Please help me. What do I do for two hours? Do I just cancel the class?" But I couldn't do that because the audience came from far away and everywhere.

Then I was up on the stage and the dreaded moment had finally come when I stood in front of eighty students with no patient. That moment was one of the windstorms of my life, and it turned out to be one of the greatest lessons of my teaching about death and dying.

I asked this mixed group of medical students, theology students, OT, RT, nurses, clergy and rabbis, "You know, we don't have a patient today. Why don't we view the biggest problem we have here in this medical school and then use that problem instead of talking to a patient." I was wondering what the group would come up with. I was just gambling to kill those two hours. Much to my surprise they picked the head of one of the departments — where all the patients died. I am not saying what this department was because then the man would be recognizable.

The Schnook

The problem this physician had was that he was trained like all the rest of us: to cure, to treat, to prolong life, but he had never gotten any help beyond that. And all his patients died.

His patients were so full of metastases you could feel the tumors getting bigger and bigger. And he had developed such a defensiveness that he went too far, and told them that they were free of cancer, and that their feelings of being ill were all in their mind.

He did this to such an extent that many of his patients asked to see a psychiatrist, because if it was all in their mind, then they needed psychiatric help.

I was in charge of the psychosomatic service. I was supposed to help those patients get rid of their fear that they were full of cancer. But I could look at the X-rays and see that they were right. They did have cancer. I think you realize the horrible conflict which he put *m e* in. *I* couldn't say, "It is not you but your doctor who needs a shrink." Of course I couldn't do that. *You can never help somebody by knocking somebody else. (silence from audience)*

And in an institution you have to have a certain degree of solidarity, so I couldn't tell this doctor that it was his problem...

So he was the doctor that they picked as a problem. And then I didn't know what to do with it. I absolutely... I was up on that stage with eighty people staring at me, and I thought, "What am I going to do now?"

I told them that I ... with this man... that you cannot help somebody if you feel locked with negativity towards him. There has to be some compassion or understanding or love, or at least understanding or liking of a person in order to help him. But if you are so negative that you would strangle this guy, and I would have loved to strangle him a thousand times, you cannot help him. So I told them that this could not be a patient that I could accept as a psychiatrist.

And then I asked a question to this group who consisted of clergy, rabbis, doctors, nurses, all helping professionals, "Who in this group likes him? Can those who like him put their hands up?" *Nobody* put their hands up!

And I got so desperate, and I looked at everybody and said, "doesn't anybody like him just a little bit?" At that time a young woman put her hand up. And without realizing it I must have attacked that poor young nurse, I guess... *(laughter from audience)* ...

because I looked at her and said, "Are you sick?" *(big laughter from audience)* You understand, in those days I believed that you must be sick to be able to like such a man.

Then we had an incredible discussion about how we are very discriminatory because we have all the love and tenderness and compassion for dying patients only. But if we would use just one inch of this love for our other fellow men, it would be marvelous. If I could be that generous and loving and understanding to these dreadful doctors whom I have to work with, *(no applause!)* maybe we could bring about some changes.

I asked this nurse, "How come you, of all the people present, like this man?" I mean there was nothing likable about him as far as I was concerned in my own old, judgmental attitude.

She was quite serious, this very young nurse. She stood up and... very calmly, not arrogantly or as a show-off, she just looked down — very modest and humble, she looked at all of us and said, "You don't know that man. You don't know this person." And *I* wanted to say, "Come on, I have worked with this idiot." *(she grumbles in mock arrogance)* But I didn't say it. I just tried to really listen to what this woman had to say because she must know something about him that I didn't know. And she shared.

She said, "You don't understand. I'm there at night. This man always comes to make his rounds at night. When everybody else is gone, he comes and makes his rounds. He comes in in this arrogant manner. He walks in like this, like a big-shot.

"He walks into a patient's room, and when he comes out his face drops. Then he goes into the next room, and when he comes out his face is longer. By the time he comes out of the last room, he looks devastated."

And she shared his physical anguish, how he, by the time he reaches the nursing station at the end of his rounds, comes out a crushed human being. And she said, "This goes on night after night after night. Sometimes I have this incredible urge to just walk over to him and touch him and say: 'God, it must be difficult!' But, naturally, in the medical hierarchy I can't do that."

So we asked, "Why not? If you can stop thinking for one moment and allow your intuition to speak and do what needs to be done, what comes to you, not evaluating and judging and criticizing it up here, *(indicating intellectual quadrant)* but instead, doing what comes to you, then you might be able to help this man. And if you help *one* man you will help thousands and thousands of people."

By the time she finished, everybody had such love and compassion for this schnook! I was embarrassed.

Then we had a big, hot discussion in this room with eighty people of all different professional levels. And we said, we really knew... and we knew that we didn't just want to pass the buck, we knew that this nurse would be the only person who could help this physician.

And she reacted in a predictable manner, like they used to do thirty years ago and sometimes are still doing, "Oh, I'm only a nurse and this is a big-shot." And we said, "It's totally irrelevant who you are in terms of academic level. Because you really have a glimpse of love for this person. You will be the one who can help him." She said, "I can't do it, I can't do it."

At the end of the class — this is probably one of the best classes I ever had because *I* learned a lot — we said, "If you ever again feel like it, you can just go and touch him. Nobody expects you to take that bigshot into your arms. But just touch him. And say whatever comes out." She didn't promise a thing. She didn't say yes or anything like it. She said, "I'll try." We left it at that.

Three days later somebody dashed into my office — fortunately I had no patient in there — laughing and crying and shouting, "I did it, I did it, I did it!"

I had no idea who she was *(laughter from audience)*. I had no idea *what* she had done. I thought she'd gone berserk. Then I recognized her and she shared her story.

That same night this guy came again, and for two nights she tried but she just didn't have the guts. But the third night, when he came out of his last room belonging to a dying young cancer patient, she suddenly remembered what she had made a commitment to do, and her intellectual quadrant started to interfere and she said to herself, "Well, one ought not to do that." Then she said, "No, I promised not to think."

So before she started thinking she moved on her intuitive, spiritual quadrant. She said, "I just walked over to him and reached out, I didn't even physically... I think that I didn't even touch him. And I said: 'God, it must be difficult!' to him."

He grabbed her and started to sob and cry and took her into his office, and with his head in his arms, just poured out his pain, his grief, his anguish and shared with her probably more than he had shared with any other human being. He shared how for many years his friends had earned a living while he was still going to school, how he specialized, how he sacrificed, how he couldn't date, how he went into a specialty where he really, really thought that he could help somebody. At the end of the sharing he said, "And now I am the chairman of a department, and every single one of my patients dies on me." Like his total impotence. Was it worthwhile to give up his personal happiness, his relationships for this?

And all she had to do was to listen.

Do you understand that? How could you ever knock such a man?

Because of the courage of this nurse to be herself, not to think what one ought to do if one is down here and the other one is up here, but because we are all brothers and sisters, she was able for two minutes to treat him like a human being, not like Doctor Bigshot but like a human being who has the same qualities that all of us have.

One year later this man asked for consultations, but only to be given by telephone so nobody would know about it. Before this he had never asked for a consultation from the psychiatric service because he was too arrogant to acknowledge that he needed help. Three or four years later, he asked for ordinary consultations like everybody else. And eventually he became a very humble, understanding man with so much compassion for his patients.

I think it would have killed him, he would have been burned out if he hadn't asked for help.

So, it is possible to do this with a schnook like him by just finding the right nurse. And, of course, you don't have to be a nurse. And nobody is too young to help. I hope you hear that.

How many of you hated, until this workshop, some of your doctors? *(silence from audience)* Be very honest. Every time you label somebody as a schnook, or whatever word you have, you increase that person's negativity. And the nurses are mainly responsible for the doctors being so obnoxious. I'm only talking about the obnoxious doctors now, but there are naturally also some good ones. Do you understand why I say that?

Because if a doctor is insecure in the first place and therefore thinks that he has to be very angry and act as a bigshot, and if he works in a unit where there are ten nurses who really hate his guts, then he will pick up their negativity, and that, in turn, will add to his insecurity. And that makes him become ten times more arrogant. Do you understand how powerful your thoughts are?

So if you think, "I'm gonna call this man a schnook again because he didn't do things my way," then immediately block those thoughts and surround him with love and understanding and compassion instead.

If a whole unit of staff will do that with one doctor for one week, you can actually see the change of that person's behavior without your ever saying one single word to him aloud. Have any of you ever tried that? You have no idea how powerful your thoughts are.

So if you surround such people — and the worst people naturally need it the most — with love and positive thoughts you can change the most impossible...

Do you hear what I am trying to say to you? This is the only way that you can bring about a change. And I will briefly talk as a psychiatrist because it is very important that you heal the world soon, before it is too late: *you have to understand that you cannot heal the world without healing yourself first.*

⚜

This is what we are talking about: unfinished business. God created man perfect, to give him all the awareness he can tolerate, all the things he can use. If you cannot tolerate it, you would not be given it. You always get what you need, but not always what you want. And as you grow and evolve, you get more. Not when you want it, but when you are ready for it.

Every human being consists of four quadrants: a physical, an emotional, an intellectual and a spiritual, intuitive quadrant.

Intellectually most of us are hypertrophic — especially in this room *(a few surprised giggles from audience)*. Spiritually we are OK. The only quadrant you never have to work with is your spiritual quadrant. It is within you and the most important reason it is not emerging is that it is blocked. Physically all of you belong to health clubs and try to do yoga exercises and eat vitamins and do all the right things, so I am not too worried about that. Our society's biggest problem is the emotional quadrant. The second developmental stage is the emotional quadrant which develops almost exclusively between the ages of one and six. That is when you get all your basic attitudes which ruin you for life. With the emphasis on "ruin."

If you live in harmony between the physical, emotional, intellectual and spiritual quadrants, you will not get sick. You can only get sick for three kinds of reasons: traumatic reasons, genetic reasons, and disharmony among the four quadrants. And I will talk about that, and it is relevant in healing, because by knowing that, you cannot only heal people but also prevent ill health. And I hope that in the next generation we will spend ninety percent of our energy in preventing ill-health rather than putting Band-Aids on something that could have been prevented in the first place.

❧

When you have children that cannot speak anymore or children who are too young, we use drawings to understand their symbolic language. I will share with you what medicine is going to be like in the next five years in terms of healing, done with a box of Crayola — as an adjunct, not the only thing.

When a child is unable to speak and I need to know what he needs to know to finish his unfinished business, I will give him a sheet of paper and a box of Crayola and ask him to draw a picture. And you do not tell the child what to draw.

In five or ten minutes you know that he knows that he is dying. You know where the pathology is. If he, for example, has a brain tumor, it will be located in a certain area of the picture. You know approximately how much time he has left and also if he is going downhill or uphill and you know his unfinished business.

We have done this with thousands of children. We have even done it with children who later were murdered and with children who later were killed by sharks or by other accidents. Much of their awareness of their impending death is subconscious, coming from the spiritual quadrant.

The reason why children always know better than grownups is that they have not yet been contaminated by negativity. If you raised the next generation with unconditional love and no punishment *ever*, but firm, consistent discipline, your next generation would need practically no healers because they would be able to heal themselves. They would be whole the way God created all of us.

You are always whole if you are in harmony between the physical, the intellectual, the emotional and the spiritual quadrants. You will experience traumas, naturally, and genetic defects will still be there.

If you raised children only with the natural emotions, and allowed them to externalize their pain, their anger, their grief, they would love to go to school. Learning would be a stimulating, challenging, exciting adventure, and the lessons would become very spiritual, because all this is within you. You are born from God, and your spiritual quadrant you don't have to shop for, pray for. It's given to you, it's a free gift. The only thing that blocks you from using it is your own negativity.

If it is indeed true that all children have all knowledge within — from your God inside of you, from your spiritual quadrant — then why do not grownups have it? How can we use this knowledge of children to help grownups?

I will now give you my favorite example to show in what sense the teaching of the symbolic language can be used to help grownups. I am using the example of cancer though I emphasize that in working with dying patients you should not emphasize cancer patients alone. People who have neurological diseases, multiple sclerosis, amyotrophic lateral sclerosis, people who have had strokes and can't speak or move anymore need just as much if not *more* help. We always talk of cancer patients as if cancer was the greatest tragedy in the world. I hope that you understand that I mean that we should help not only cancer patients but *all* people.

Bernie Siegel

We had a physician who came to our workshop who was very impressed with our use of spontaneous drawings with dying children. About two years ago he had the courage to be labeled a fool, to be called — he is called now a heretic... he is called... well, he got another nice label. We challenged him by sharing with him that we truly believe that this gift of inner knowledge is true not only with terminally ill children but also with entirely healthy grownups. After the diagnosis of a potentially terminal illness is verified, you simply ask the patient to draw a picture — no instructions, nothing else — just to give you an impression of where this person is at this time. Then after you have this impression you ask them to conceive of their cancer.

This physician took those drawings, went home and said, "OK, I will try to do what you say works."

Instead of telling his cancer patients what they ought to do, he gives them unconditional love and respect. And he puts no expectations on them and no claims. He says to his patients, "draw me a picture!" The patients draw a picture, and then he knows where they are at, not only from the physical quadrant, but also from the emotional, spiritual, intellectual quadrants.

My dream picture — I have to brag about that — was a man who was diagnosed as having cancer *(shows a drawing to audience)*, and I will describe it for those of you who can't see it. After the patient had drawn a general picture — from which you can make a general evaluation of him — he was asked to conceive of his cancer. He drew a man — I am only drawing a symbolic body here — and in his body he drew big red concentric circles, meaning a body full of big red (danger color) cancer cells.

When he was asked to conceive of chemotherapy, which in this case was the treatment of choice that the oncologist had elected, and which I think most physicians would have recommended in this case, he drew big black arrows, each arrow hitting a cancer cell.

But there was a very odd and unexpected thing about his drawing. As the chemotherapy black arrows hit those red cancer cells each arrow deflected away from it.

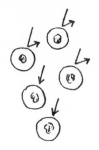

Chemotherapy

If you didn't know anything about the interpretation of drawings and you were this patient's physician, would you have put him on chemotherapy? Would you have regarded him as a good candidate for this kind of treatment?

This patient was considered to be a good candidate for chemotherapy. Nevertheless, something inside this man — but not his intellect — told me that internally he knew that he was going to reject the chemotherapy that was offered him.

Now, the patient's message comes from a quadrant that is not yet considered reality by most of humanity. Because from our own intellectual, hypertrophic quadrant that considers itself to know everything better than the patient does, we consider this man to be silly, because it is statistically verified that this cancer responds beautifully to this type of chemotherapy. Therefore, the patient should be given it.

But when you look at what the patient's intuitive quadrant is saying, you can see that in this case chemotherapy just won't work.

So unconditional love — love which is not schmaltzy and sentimental — means: I respect my neighbor as myself. I respect people who have a knowledge about themselves that is beyond *my* knowledge of them. *Their* knowledge comes from a different quadrant but nevertheless it is always more accurate than what comes from the intellectual quadrant.

If I can respect that and know that, I can ask this man, "What did your doctor tell you about this chemotherapy?" This man answers, "My doctor told me that the chemotherapy kills my cancer cells." And I say, "*Yes!*" meaning, "Go on, get it!" And his face drops.

I think that I am missing something, so again I say, "What did your doctor tell you about the chemotherapy?" Again he says very matter of factly, "My doctor told me that the chemotherapy kills my cancer cells."

And this time I say, "Yes, *but...?*"

He looks at me as if he wants to check me out, and he says, "Thou shalt not kill."

And I say, "Huh?"

He repeats again, "Thou shalt not kill."

And now — understanding better — I say, "Not even your own cancer cells?" and he says, "No. You see Doctor Ross, I was raised as a Quaker. I truly believe in universal law: Thou shalt not kill. And I was thinking about it very seriously: No, I do not think that I can kill."

If you practice unconditional love, you respect your fellow man without trying to convince, convert or change him. So I had no problem telling him that I wished all people would believe in universal law, because then the world would be a very peaceful and beautiful place. This was an implicit expression of my respect for him and made it clear to him that I was not going to belittle him, laugh at him or criticize him. But then I had to add, "Do me a favor." You understand, I want all my patients to get well. I am not saying that to him, but that is what I am now trying to talk him into. I say, "Do me a favor. Go home, and conceive how you can get rid of your cancer." Do you understand the difference in wording? And he says, "That is a good idea."

And he leaves and a week later he comes back.

I ask him, "Were you able to conceive a way to get rid of your cancer, which really means how *we* can help you?" And he has again that gorgeous smile on his face. And he says, "Yep!" I said, "Draw me a picture!"

And his whole picture — and I am only drawing a single big one so you can see what it looked like — instead of being full of red cancer cells, the whole body of the man that he drew was now full of gnomes. These little guys, you know... *(draws a gnome at the blackboard. Amusement from audience)* ... every gnome was lovingly carrying away a cancer cell *(applause and happy laughter)*.

The Gnomes

I was very touched by him. I called his oncologist and told him this, and on the very same day, he put the patient on chemotherapy. Today this man is still well.

Do you see the beauty of this? It is to me an incredible opening of things. It only takes humility, the only thing it takes is to know that all of us have all the knowledge we need within, and if we are humble and open and respect and love our neighbors as ourselves, we can help each other.

And it doesn't take time. It takes five minutes and doesn't cost a nickel. I am not exaggerating.

I hope you understand that this is what we consider holistic medicine. I may have the intellectual knowledge of the malignancy. The patient has his intuitive knowledge. And if we begin to work together and respect and help each other, then we can truly help each other to become whole.

This is to me what healing is in our time. In some way it has to do with consciousness and I don't know how to put that. It has to do with openness. And you cannot be open and you cannot reach this knowledge and this understanding and this compassion and this unconditional love as long as you have a Hitler within you. So, doctor: *Heal thyself!* And you are all doctors. All of you have to have the humility to acknowledge all the negativity that you have inside of yourself, every day.

And if you could do that, if you could acknowledge what I learned in Maidanek...It was in Maidanek that the woman stepped out who had lost her entire family. It was she who said to me, "Don't you believe, Elisabeth, that in all of us there is a Hitler?"

Yes. And in all of us is also a Mother Theresa. You cannot become a Mother Theresa, symbolically speaking, if you do not have the courage to look at your Hitler and get rid of him.

So this is what I say to you: if you want to *heal* the world, then heal yourself, get rid of your Hitler within. Then you will become a whole human being the way God created you. Then you will have cosmic consciousness, you will have out of body experiences, you will have anything you need — but not what you want, thank God *(amusement from audience).*

The Workshops

Some people asked about the workshops. The workshops are offered by Shanti Nilaya. We give workshops all over the world from California to Australia. We invite seventy-five people to spend one week with us, from Monday noon till Friday noon. About one third of them are terminally ill patients or parents of dying children, one third are physicians, clergy, social workers, counselors, nurses, and one third are regular people. And what we do with this group is to show all the participants how in five days they can look at their own unfinished business and get rid of it. And you understand, the younger you are when you do it the more fully you can live afterwards.

It's a very intense five day workshop, where usually the terminally ill patients begin to share their anguish and pain and their unfinished business, their grief, and they touch upon their own pool of repressed tears and anger and unfinished business. And then we help them to ventilate it and externalize it. And on the last night, Thursday night, we have a very moving ritual, where people are in front of an outdoor fireplace, usually with their own wine and bread, and they share with the group what they are willing to leave behind. And they do that symbolically with a pine cone, placing the negativity into it and throwing it into the fire.

When we have the courage to look at our own negativity and leave it behind, then we can become more like Mother Theresa. You cannot sit on your negativity and think that you can meditate it away. That really does not work.

You will find more pain and anguish in a group of seventy-five people than you can ever imagine, once you don't see the front but what is deep down inside that pool of repressed anguish and agony. And the greatest grief you can ever experience, which is far greater than any loss that anybody ever talks about, is *the grief over love that you have never experienced.* That is the greatest grief. Most people in our society have never experienced unconditional love, except perhaps from a Grandma or a Grandpa.

The last five-day workshop, from which I am just coming, had seventeen suicidal patients, who came to the workshop as their last straw, with a threat that if it didn't help they would commit suicide. I told them not to do it before Friday afternoon *(laughter from audience).* That too is something that you have to take seriously, but you also have to make these people aware that we human beings are totally and solely and exclusively responsible for our own lives. So don't go around and cry on other people's shoulders and waste your energy on self-pity. It is you and your choices that bring you where you are at.

And we human beings should bless ourselves every single day because we are the only living creatures in this galaxy who have been given free choice. And after death, when most of you for the first time realize what life *here* is all about, you will begin to see that your life here is almost nothing but the sum total of every choice you have made during every moment of your life. Your thoughts, which you are responsible for, are as real as your deeds. You will begin to realize that every word and every deed affect your life and also touch thousands of other lives.

Christ

Just watch yourself when you get up in the morning and are grouchy. You make your husband or your wife miserable and they go to work and let it out on the secretary. Then the secretary lets it out on her husband. Your children go to school miserable. They kick the dog on their way out, beat up the other kids and end up in the principal's office. You should count once how one grouch getting up in the morning can make life miserable for so many people.

It is such little things that you can experiment with yourself. The next day — even if you feel grouchy — sing, yodel or whistle just long enough until they are out of the house *(laughter)*. And then you may beat a rubber hose on a mattress and let out your anger on an inanimate object.

And then at the end of the day, ask your spouse, your mate, your children what kind of a day they have had, and then you will begin to see that *you* can change your life with simple things. You do not need to go to India, and you do not need LSD or mescaline or psilocybin in order to change your life. And you do not need to do anything except to be responsible for your choices.

And do what Christ did after what the Bible calls "fighting Satan," which was nothing but fighting the Hitler within himself after the forty days of fasting. He was totally aware that he could be the ruler of Jerusalem, that he could change this very decadent place at that time. But he also knew that it would not last long. The highest choice that he had available was to be willing never to use his powers and to be willing even to give his life if he could help one fellow man to understand that death does not exist, that death is only a transition to a different form of living.

He did that very thing. He knew that people believed in him only as long as he performed miracles. The moment he disappeared they would start wondering again. He knew the difference between knowing and believing.

And so after his death he materialized for his friends and his disciples for three days and three nights. He ate with them, he talked to them, he shared with them. And then they knew.

And it was the knowing, not the believing, that gave them the courage to do what they needed to do.

Those of you who are willing to go through the forty days of fasting, symbolically speaking — that means going through hell, being labeled, ridiculed, knocked, criticized — and in spite of that take the highest choice, you will not regret it.

And again, to give you a *very* practical example:

Dougy again

A couple of years ago I went to visit a nine-year-old boy in Virginia who was dying of cancer. And before I left I told him that he must have many questions. I said, "I cannot make house calls in Virginia very often but if you have any questions, just write to me."

One day I got a letter from Dougy. The letter was a two liner, "Dear Dr. Ross, I have only one more question left. What is life and what is death and why do little children have to die? Love, Dougy."

Do you understand why I am prejudiced in favor of children? They cut through all the baloney *(laughter from audience)*. So I wrote him a letter. And I couldn't write him, you know, big stuff. I had to write to him the way he wrote to me.

So I wrote like that. I used those gorgeous felt pencils that have twenty-eight colors, rainbow colors. And it didn't look right yet so I started to illustrate it. Then when it was finished I liked it so much I wanted to keep it. My rationalization was naturally, "Yes, you are entitled to keep it. You know, you really worked on this letter, and it soon will be five o'clock, and the post office will be closed, and your children will come home from school, and you'd better put dinner up," and all the excuses why it was OK to do that — to keep the letter. The longer the list of excuses, the more I knew that it was *not* OK. So I said, "Here I go round teaching always to take the highest choice. What is my highest choice now? My highest choice is to go right down to the post office and to let go of it, because I did it for him, not for me." So I walked to the post office and mailed it.

Dougy was very proud and very happy. He shared it with many other dying children. That, in itself would have been very beautiful.

But about five months later, in March, when his birthday came up, this rather poor family made a long distance phone call to me. Dougy got on the phone and said, "Dr. Ross, today is my birthday. You are the only one who had enough faith that I would have another birthday. And I need to give you a gift for my birthday. I couldn't think of what to give you. We have nothing. The only thing that comes to me"... ("the only thing that comes to me," that is the spiritual quadrant)... "the only thing that comes to me over and over is to give you your beautiful letter back *(happy laughter from audi-*

ence). But on one condition!" (it wasn't unconditional love!) *(laughter from audience)* "On one condition: that you print it *(laughter from audience)* and make it available to other dying children."

A lot of things started to rush through my head: it is expensive, twenty-eight colors on each page *(laughter from audience)*, intellectual quadrant, thrifty Swiss, how can people afford it. All that was interfering so I said, "No!" to it. Instead I took the highest choice. And it is literally true: if you share of yourself without expectations you get back ten thousand times.

This was four and a half years ago. When Dougy died, the *Dougy Letter* had reached ten thousand dying children *(applause)*.

Differentiate between your intellect and your intuition. When you think, it is your intellect. *(laughter)* When you do what *feels* right, it is your intuition. Intuition comes fast, makes no sense, is totally illogical and feels terrific *(happy laughter and applause)*. If you follow your intuition you are always in trouble. But I have a favorite thing at Shanti Nilaya which I believe in more than I believe in anything else and that is: *"Should you shield the canyons from the windstorms you will never see the beauty of their carvings."*

And when you follow your intuition you become a canyon eventually — if you last. But it is wonderful. *(in a happy, peaceful voice)*: I would not like to live in any other time, because it was never more difficult and never more rewarding.

Elisabeth Kübler-Ross on farm with llamas

To Say Yes to It

Good Friday

Seven years ago to the day I was here the last time. And to me it is very significant. Seven is a very significant number anyway. And Easter is the most important day in our lives — whether you know it or not.

Seven years ago I was here, talking to a group of people. I didn't know then that I was seven years ahead of my heavenly schedule. It didn't work out. And I am very glad that I didn't know seven years ago what was coming. Because then I would have hung myself on the next Christmas tree *(laughter from audience)*.

Every day in my life — and that to me is what Good Friday is all about — Good Friday is viewed by many people as a sad day because of the crucifixion. But without the crucifixion we wouldn't have had the resurrection. And without the windstorms in life my patients would not die with peace and dignity and really knowing what we all need to know at the moment of our death. And so, today I want to talk mainly about the windstorms of life, the purpose of the windstorms of life, and how you should raise your children so they are not afraid of living or of dying.

I'm *not* the "death and dying lady." I hope in the next fifty years I will be known as the "life and living lady"! Because if you live right you will never, ever be afraid to die. *Dying is the greatest pleasure that awaits you.* You should never be worried about that. Instead you should be worried about what you do today. If today you take your highest choice in everything, not just in your deeds but also in your words and your thoughts, then you will have a most incredibly blissful moment at the moment of your death.

All we need to learn is how to raise one generation of youngsters with real unconditional love and firm consistent discipline. There is an old saying somewhere in the Bible — and I never quote that right but you know what I am talking about — the father's sins will be passed on to his children and children's children. That simply means that if you were beaten or if you were sexually abused as a child — a minimum of twenty-five percent of our population grow up with incest — if you were beaten as a kid then you, in your turn, will beat *your* children, because of all the anguish and frustration and the impotent rage which is still inside of you. And if you are not helped to get all this pain out before you are grownups and have your own kids, you will pass this on to the next generation. So I think it is our generation's duty to practice what was taught two thousand years ago: Love thy neighbor as thyself!

And we have to start with ourselves because we cannot love others if we don't love ourselves. And we can never trust others if we cannot trust ourselves. So when I talk about how to raise the next generation, I mean that we have to begin with ourselves, and then it becomes easier and easier and easier.

God created man with five natural emotions. Learn to respect those five natural emotions and don't turn them into unnatural emotions. It is these unnatural emotions which later give you all your unfinished business.

Anger is a natural, God-given gift that, in its natural form, takes fifteen seconds. Fifteen seconds is enough time to say, "No thank you."

And if children are not allowed to express their own assertiveness and authority and natural anger they will end up as Hitlers, small or big Hitlers, full of rage and revenge and hate. The world is full of them.

Grief is a natural emotion which helps you to take care of all the losses in life. How many of you were allowed to cry as little children? If you have a Swiss mother who is very neat and clean and your security blanket gets a little washed out and she says: "Shame!" and she throws it out, it is a horrible loss for a little child. And if you are not allowed to cry or if you are told, "If you don't stop crying I will give you something to cry about, that will shut you up very fast," then you'll rather be quiet than get a spanking. And then, when you grow up, you will have lots of problems with self-pity. You will literally marinate in self-pity. You will not be good at hospice work or helping anybody. You will have lots of shame and guilt.

When you go and watch films like "E.T.," you can see all this shame and guilt by watching the audience. When the light comes on during the break, a lot of people clean their glasses explaining it away by saying that they have become foggy. And that is because they are ashamed to admit that they have cried. This is unfinished business: *you fear that you are not allowed to grieve.*

Love is unconditional. Love has no claims, no expectations. It just *is.*

One form of natural love is holding and hugging the baby, who then feels nurtured and cared for. Another form of love is to be able to say "No." And that is very hard for a lot of people. If you can say to a boy, "I'm not gonna tie your shoe laces. I have all the confidence in the world that you can do that on your own," then he might have a temper tantrum or he might really try to manipulate you. Then you will have to *stick* to it and to convey to him, "I trust that you can do it by yourself. I trust that you can do it even better than I did it at your age." Then he will bend down and try his best, and he will be *so* proud when he finds out that he can learn how to tie his shoelaces himself.

This develops self-trust and self-love. It is very, very important that you know this and if you have any unfinished business, get rid of it, because if you don't, it will not only bug you for the rest of your life, but it will grow like a tapeworm and will eventually suffocate you internally.

When you lose somebody and you have lived fully, you will have no grief *work* whatsoever. You will have a lot of *grief* , but no grief *work.*

Grief *work* is *unfinished business.* It is fear, shame and guilt and all unnatural emotions, and all unfinished business, and all this will naturally drain your energy and decrease your sense of wholeness and health.

Suicide Out of Free Choice

You and you alone are responsible for your choices. But by making the choice you also have to accept the responsibility. Say that someone wants to take his life. When he makes that decision, then he also has to accept the consequences of his choices. And that means he is going to put a *lot* of guilt on his relatives, and a lot of "Why did it happen?" and "What did I do wrong?" and "Why didn't I pick up the cues?," and, you know, all the things that make this situation into a nightmare. And *he* will be responsible for putting *them* through the nightmare. And that is his... load, that he has to bring with him to the other side.

So any time you make a choice, make sure you have the right to make a free choice. It is man's biggest gift that we were given at birth as human beings. We are the only creatures in the Universe, as far as we know, who have been given free choice. But with that goes also a *lot* of responsibility.

And then you really have to differentiate. I would say probably seventy percent of all young people who commit suicide are the physician's responsibility, and that is the only way I can put it: Do we have any psychiatrists in this group? Yes!

Because we really do have to diagnose beginning episodes of undiagnosed manic depressives. We do not diagnose that enough. If a young person is very depressed —well maybe she has lost her boyfriend or she has had a fight or a struggle with her father or mother — we regard that as normal. We do not detect early signs of very, very frequent undiagnosed manic depressives. And the only thing that those patients would need is to be put on Lithium. Lithium is the only thing that I know that is working with these patients. It can take the edge off the depression. They will *still* get depressed but they will reach a certain bottom line and then not go any further. And if they go high, they will still go high but not too high, which they do when they are totally out of control.

And so we have to educate the population much, much more about first episodes of manic depressive psychosis and put the patients on the right medication. I am not a psychiatrist that puts people on lots of drugs. Lithium is one of the few drugs that I use.

It is a very different issue in terms of the consequences of choices if, for example, a young girl commits suicide because of a boyfriend or a mother and she is just furious, "How dare you do that to me? *I* am going to make you so guilty you will be sorry for the rest of your life." Then she commits suicide as an act of revenge, to make somebody else feel *really* guilty. And she pays with her life — she is so furious she would do anything to make the boyfriend feel awful, as an example of how he made *her* feel. This reason for committing suicide has very, very different consequences than if somebody is an undiagnosed manic depressive and is so depressed that no matter what you say or do, she wants nothing else but to end her life. And no matter what you say, you cannot get her out of it.

Suicide as a Result of an Endogenous Depression

How many of you have once felt really, really hopelessly depressed? Then you know what it is like. If you multiply this by ten, then you will know what a manic-depressive feels in his or her depression. Nothing makes any sense, nothing! It's... it's worse than nothing. It's total vacuum. There is absolutely no way of getting out into the sunshine. And for the depressed person, the only solution is to end it all like this, because it has become unbearable.

You understand that at the end, when you do the life review after you die, that will be evaluated as if you had died of cancer. That form of depression and suicide is an illness that you are not held responsible for.

❦

You cannot "graduate" until you have learned all the lessons that you came to learn in this life time, and also until you have taught the things that you came to teach. Life is nothing but a school, literally a school where you are tested, where you have to pass your tests. And if you pass your tests you get a double whopper. If you pass that next test, which is much tougher than the first one, then you get a triple whopper. And it goes on and on and on, but it doesn't get easier. It gets worse! It gets harder and tougher each time, but it also *comes* easier. Do you understand what I mean? It is like giving math problems for a fifth grader to a first grader: it would be impossible for him. But to give those problems to a fifth grader is a different thing. By fifth grade he is already better prepared and he will have a fair chance to make it.

When you think that you have really made it to the top of the mountain, and that you can really take it now, then you get the two-by-four over you head *(knowing laughter from audience)*. If you get the two-by-four over your head and you survive, then you get... I don't know what's the next size to a two-by-four? But you get a big stick over your head. How many of you have gone through at least a two by four stage? *(answer from audience, "I think that I have done that.")* Did you think that it was tough? *("Yes!")* Well, then the best is yet to come! *(laughter from audience)*

That's what life is all about. The sole purpose of life is spiritual evolution: to grow until you are so perfect that they can put you through a tumbler. And you know that when you are put into that tumbler of life, which is symbolically speaking, your choice — and *nobody else's* choice — you come out either crushed or polished.

The Difference Between Rescue and Help

When you accomplice somebody's rescue you are not helping. You all understand that on some level. Because if you rescue someone you make *him* weak and *you* will be the bigshot. If you rescue him and Band-Aid him, you don't help him at all.

We are all our brother's keepers and our sister's keepers. We are responsible to help wherever it is needed. But you have to know the difference between *rescuing* somebody: trying to fix something in somebody else's life, and *helping* him: to be available when that person has learned to be humble enough to ask for help. It is a very thin line between being a rescuer and being a real helper, a decent human being.

(Someone in the audience asks Elisabeth what to do when somebody who is very ill says that he doesn't want to live anymore.) Did anyone talk to you about the universal laws? You need to know some very basic universal laws. *Thou shalt not kill* is an absolute universal law, and that goes for all mankind. It is not only for our own religion but for every single one of them. If somebody asks you to kill him, no matter for what reason, you first have to find out why he doesn't want to live anymore. How many of you are taking care of people who don't want to live, who are tied down to a chair, incontinent, who stare into space, and nobody kisses them or touches them?

How many of you would like to exist that way? Nobody, of course. If you know... if you can really identify with that person, "I wouldn't like to exist that way," then ask yourself, "What can I do to change his situation so that he can not only exist until he dies, but can really live until he dies?" Then you go about changing this or that for him.

How many of you have seen Katie's film that we made about dancing with old people who were all paralyzed and in wheel chairs? You have not seen it?

We have a video tape we made on how to help old people — and on purpose you pick *very* old people, not sixty-two year olds, so we don't have to think that they could be us *(laughter from audience)*. You take a group of eighty- to one-hundred-and-four-year-old women and men in a nursing home who are all paralyzed and in wheel chairs. And typically very old, a very helpless kind of not very peppy old people — and try to teach them how to live.

We got this dancer who showed them how to dance. And they were all paralyzed you understand, and in wheel chairs. So she put the wheel chairs in a circle and we had a photographer who took a video of what we were doing with those people. But he didn't do it like we would do it, where the people show off in front of the camera, smiling and trying to look sweet and happy. No, he had the camera behind them and he just photographed their feet, dead feet, just hanging there. And then as she danced — and she used Tchaikovsky and Mozart and all the old classical music — you suddenly began to see the foot moving *(amazement from audience)*. And then you see, they are really going. And you saw an old man just bounce, starting to fiddle around with the woman next to him (*big laughter from audience*) and started to grab and started to touch. And things were happening, and on this film you can see all this.

And the old man got engaged to that old lady later on (*happy laughter*). And she insisted that she would be his bride, but she only wanted to be his bride because she wanted a new dress! (*laughter*) I mean, a shrewd old lady (*big laughter*).

You should see this film. And you should see this nursing home. (*Question from audience, "What is the name of that nursing home?"*) I have had a stroke, I have no more memory. But the video tape is in the news letter. Something about dancing with old ladies. And they dance like you wouldn't believe it. And all with one person who plays the right music and brings life into that life.

My Mother

When my mother was old she had one really big hang-up: she could not receive. She would give her shirt away; she could do anything for anybody. She worked her butt off all her life. She raised triplets and a six-year-old boy and you know what it was like sixty years ago to raise triplets. You didn't have a laundry machine, you didn't have Pampers, you didn't have hot water. She had to nurse us for nine months every three hours day and night and it was tough. But she gave and she gave and she was all love.

But she could not take anything. She could not do that. I mean she was pathological!

If a neighbor would bake a pie on Saturday and bring it to her just to give her a break and have some dessert ready, the next weekend she had to bake a pie and bring back to her neighbor.

Do you know people like this? Would you please tell them my story so they don't end up the same way? I myself have to learn the same thing.

She was terribly afraid that one day she would end up as a vegetable because she would then be *totally doomed* to receive. That was absolutely the worst thing that could ever happen in her life. And we always pulled her leg and said, "You are going to be sorry if you can't just gracefully accept it. You make this woman happy by accepting the pie." But she couldn't hear.

She was afraid of becoming a vegetable, and one day we got a phone call saying that Mama had been found in the bathroom with a massive stroke. She was paralyzed, unable to speak, unable to move anything, unable to do anything.

We rushed her to the hospital. The only part she was able to move was her left hand a little bit. And because she tried to use her left hand to pull the tube out of her nose — she needed that tube naturally — they tied that hand down, and that one became totally useless too. So she couldn't move one-tenth of an inch of her body. And I promised her, "I'll help you to live until you die."

But I could not help her to die. Already, sometime *before* the stroke, she begged me to give her something if she ever became a vegetable. And I said, "I can't do that. How can I do that to a mother who kept me alive by nursing me every three hours, day and night, with all the sacrifice, and now I should.... Really, I can't do that." She was furious with me.

I made a mistake then — she was in her full senses — when I said, "I can't help you to die but I will help you to live until you die." I knew that she was pissed at me and not happy and could not understand and she said, "You are the only doctor in the family, it would be very easy."

I did not buy it, thank God, and I am a softy.

Three days after this discussion I was back in America and got the phone call from home that she had been found with a massive stroke. I immediately returned to Switzerland.

We rushed her to the hospital where they had a respirator ready and the whole works. And she used — you know now what the rubber hose is,[1] right? — she used the aluminum side rail as her rubber hose.

She rattled that aluminum side rail so you could hear it outside the hospital. When you came in you could hear the rattle and the rage. You know, she couldn't speak, so this was her only way of

---

[1] In Elisabeth's workshops the participants learn to beat a mattress with a piece of rubber hose in order to facilitate the expression of pain, rage and impotence.

expressing herself. I knew that I couldn't stand listening to that sound although I understood her rage. She was totally impotent and she just had to let people wash her, feed her, take care of everything for her.

And so I asked her if she wanted me to take her to the equivalent of a hospice. This was a long time ago when they didn't have hospices. But what I had in mind was an old... it's like where nuns take care of patients and just love them. No machines, no respirators, no nothing. And she said yes, she would like that. That was her real, clear message.

In Switzerland, it's very hard to find decent places like that because you have a waiting list for two or three years. And that was the only time when I was grateful that I was a triplet, that we were three people who could put our heads together to find a place for her. One of my sisters is *very* seductive, the other one is a real politician, and I came from America, which means I have money *(laughter from audience)*. This was a long time ago when a dollar was one to four.

I was supposed to pay for whatever it cost, my seductive sister was going to try to seduce the doctor *(laughter)* to give her a bed, and the politician was allowed to use any dirty tricks *(laughter)*. Who do you think got the bed within forty-eight hours? *(answer from audience, "The dollar?")*

Not in *Switzerland*, thank God *(big laughter)*. The seductive one! *(amazement from audience)* In forty-eight hours she had a bed! We never asked her how she did it. *(very big laughter)*

She got a bed in Basel. I had my mother in Zurich, which is, you know quite far away, and she got the bed from somebody who had just died and they just swapped the beds, got it fast.

The trip from Zurich to Basel with my mother was the best trip with any critically ill patient I've ever made in my entire life. Before the trip I had to empty her house. You know what it is like to give away anything and everything that belongs to your mother? *(with the slightest catch in her voice)* And she was still alive, but you know she can never again move into... Pictures, books, clothes, absolutely everything. This was *my* last home too, you know, so I also gave up a chance to go back home, whatever that was.

I made a list of all the things that she was attached to a little bit, like... one day we had bought her a little mink hat, the next Christmas we bought her the collar, you know. We all saved money to buy this mink hat and collar. She was so proud that she had the little mink hat, for my mother is a very modest woman.

I made a list of all those things and I rented an ambulance to take me and her from Zurich to Basel. I also bought a bottle of eggnog —spiced eggnog which is called "Ei-congnac." It is more cognac than eggs *(laughter from audience)* I don't think you have it here. It is a delicious Dutch drink. You don't know that it is booze but you *feel* it *(laughter from audience)*. None of us in the family ever drank alcohol but now I needed a bottle of egg cognac.

I and my mother went to Basel in the ambulance. I had this master list of all her things that I needed to find a home for, you know, all the things she loved. And I told her that she must make [the sound] "hrrr" when I found the right person for the right thing.

For each and every one of her things on my list I went through all the possible candidates, like the wife of the mailman and the wife of the milkman. I mentioned a name and nothing happened, and I mentioned another name and still nothing happened, and I mentioned another name and then every time I mentioned the right person she suddenly made, "Hrrr," and then I wrote down next to the hat or the collar who was to have it. And every time we hit the nail on the head we... *(demonstrates how they took a sip of egg cognac)* we had a drink *(laughter from audience)*. And by the time we arrived in Basel the bottle was empty, but *(with laughter in her voice)* the *list* was complete. That was my last finishing of unfinished business with my Mama and it was the most joyful trip I've ever had with any patient in my life.

But then she got into this hospital, which was like a two hundred years old building, and the side rails were made of hardwood and you could not move them!

In the hospital in Basel we took her "rattle" away. You know, that was her toy, her only way of expressing her rage and impotence. And *I* said, "Well, that's only gonna last for few days, and she's gonna stick it out until then."

But she *existed* this way for four years. Four years! No sound. No way to express herself. And she stared at me and I felt guilty, and she had a knack for making me feel guilty just by her looks.

I was furious with God. I cannot tell you, I could have shred Him to pieces if I'd had the chance. I used every language, Swiss, French, Italian, English, everything. He didn't budge. He gave no response. No *nothing*.

And I said to Him, "You S.O.B." *(in an angry voice)* in *our* language. And I got absolutely no reaction from Him. That made me even more furious.

You know, you can call Him every name, and He just sits there and loves you. *(She growls in mock anger. Laughter from audience).* You know, it is like when you are really mad and somebody says, "Sweetie Pie" to you *(laughter from audience)*. And you could kill Him. But He is *dead* already. You can't even kill Him. And I went through all the rage, the bargaining, the depression and the guilt trip and the whole works.

This rage of mine lasted not only for the four years that she continued *existing* in that body, but weeks and months after she died I still tried to review my opinion of God. I really needed to come to grips with this. I thought, "He can't be such an S.O.B. But how can a loving, compassionate, understanding God let this woman suffer who has been seventy-nine years loving and giving and caring and sharing?" I mean, that is not God. That's the other one, and I don't want to have anything to do with him, that was my opinion.

***

And then, months after she died — needless to say we were very relieved and glad when she finally died — I took the... I don't know how to say it, but one day I reviewed my opinion of God. And the moment I realized what this was all about I almost jumped out of my skin. And I said, "Thank you, thank you, thank you, thank you, you are the most generous man that ever existed." And I had a thing about cheap men *(laughter from audience)*. Cheap men were my hang-up in my first workshop. So to call Him a generous man was the biggest compliment I could give God *(laughter)* and it had to be a man, not a woman, because I had a hang-up with cheap men, not with cheap women. So when I *finally* did this review I jumped out of my skin, and I said, "You are the most generous man that has ever existed."

You know, what suddenly came to me on that day is that you get your lessons one way or another, you understand, and *you* yourself are responsible for what lessons you *get* — and, since I at least *knew* this, I shouldn't have had such a tough one — and at last I realized what He did for her, and that you are only able to see that from a distance. So when you sit on top, when you sit at your brother's side, you are *so* nonobjective that you cannot see. But if you go to Timbuktu or you go into the wilderness and meditate or you go to Arizona and away or whatever you do.... It takes distance to see clearly.

And with my distance from my horribly suffering mother who laid guilt trips on me with her looks, I finally saw that this is the most generous God because he allowed her to give and give and give and love for seventy-nine years and she only had to learn to receive for four years.

You understand that? Generous —

Nowadays if I see somebody who just has to learn it the hard way because he didn't learn it the easy way, I know for sure it's *His* doing. But we are not taught that. But you see, we were taught this earlier, and then we really knew that we, ourselves, are responsible for whatever we don't hear, cannot hear. This is what I meant before; you get a two-by-four over your head. If you don't acknowledge the two-by-four, then the next time you will get an even bigger stick over your head, which might even break your skull.

For about a year I was taught by my students that I had to relax, I had to learn R & R. I didn't know what R & R was. It doesn't exist in my vocabulary. No matter how often I asked, I was told that R & R meant Rest and Relaxation. Two minutes later I forgot and I kept going and going and going and didn't.

The last time I asked I was told, "You really have to relax now. Take a step out, you can't do everything, but you have to learn to rest. You cannot go on like this seventeen hours a day, seven days a week." And, yeah, I heard it, sure, and I thought to myself that when I got around to it, I would do it.

Then in August 1988 I had my stroke and I was paralyzed, and I couldn't speak.

In the beginning of December 1988, I was told that if I didn't *really* practice R & R now, I would get another... "popra" I think they called it... it's a little stroke.

If you don't learn from the first lesson, they just give you another one and a tougher one to that. So now I'm practicing R & R and this is my first workshop in ages, where I just sit in for a little while.

Now, *if* I had given my mother an overdose — to answer your question — my mother *would* have had to come back, would have had to start from scratch, and learn to receive. Maybe she would have had to be born with a spina bifida, or to be born paralyzed, or incontinent or something, so that somebody would have had to clean her "tusch"... what do you call that? Clean her...? And maybe they would also have had to feed her and do *everything* for her, so that she would be *forced* to learn to receive.

Now, by saying "NO," because I really loved her — I still do — she was spared a whole lifetime of agony. Do you understand what I mean by that?

You cannot *rescue* people, because if you do that, they will still have to learn the lesson that you rescued them from. And this is for the same reason that you cannot go into a high school exam and take somebody else's tests to get an ECFMG if you are in medical school, or a high school diploma for somebody else. They have to make it themselves. Love, real love is the answer. My teachers give me the best definition of what love is really all about — real love means that you allow them to learn their own lessons without rescuing them. Love is to know when to put training wheels on the child's bicycle and also to know when to take them off. That is love. Removing the training wheels is much more difficult than putting them on, and yet eventually you will *have* to remove them.

So if someone wants to be rescued — in this sense of the word — lovingly tell him that whatever he learns from this agony, *he* picked it in order to pass his tests, and if you fake it and make it easy for him, then you cheat him out of a quantum leap of progress and he will hate you for God knows how long for taking his last chance away to learn that particular lesson.

Do you all understand that? It is a very thin line between being a *rescuer* and being a real *helper*, a decent human being. It is very important that you understand this.

(A woman in the audience thinks that Elisabeth contradicts herself when she says that you should refrain from rescuing someone who is in a difficult situation and asks for help.)

No, you *are* allowed to go as far as to deplete your resources: if I meet somebody who has lots of pain from cancer, I put him on a painkiller. If I meet somebody whom I can verify as having an undiagnosed manic-depressive psychosis, I naturally put him on Lithium. That is as far as you're allowed to go as healthcare people. There *is* a limit to what you can gratify in terms of what they ask of you. Real love is to say, "No thank you. This is as much as I can do for you. And the rest, you have to do on your own."

Yes, it's difficult, it's not easy. There are lots of times when I don't know if it's decent to even prolong somebody's life. Maybe they will not be able to have any function at all in life and, as a physician, I was trained to use all the life supporting machines there are. And then I know that if this were me I wouldn't want that to happen. But here in America you have lawsuits. You are obliged to do it.

Number two: if there is a family member who gives you the evil eye, saying you haven't tried this and that, then you will have to decide whether you are going to gratify the patient's real needs or whether you are going to take care of that one relative who has so much unfinished business with the patient that *he* can't let him go. It is not all black and white. It is not easy at all.

Active euthanasia, in my opinionated opinion, is a one-hundred-and-fifty percent NO. Because you do not know why people have to go through that particular lesson. And if you try to rescue them, you will be cursed. Do you understand what I mean? It's very important.

(Question from audience, "Could you explain how getting rid of your unfinished business helps you grow spiritually?") To me it's the only way. How much time do you have? *(laughter from audience)* I will tell

you briefly how I got rid of my Hitler if you don't mind. It will take at least fifteen minutes.

My Father

You have to become honest. That is the absolutely basic requirement. You cannot be a phony-baloney. And I don't mean with other people but with yourself. When you get ugly, negative, angry, hateful, anything icky, then acknowledge that it is *your* stuff and not your fellow man's.

You know, I give workshops all over the world to help people get rid of their unfinished business. Years ago I was asked to go to Hawaii to give a workshop. We always look for some old convents because they have big space, a gorgeous environment, most of them are empty, they are not too expensive, and the food is halfway decent. These are our basic requirements. And also, naturally, when you scream, that the cops don't come. So it has to be really remote.

And we couldn't find a place in Hawaii. We were almost ready to give up the whole thing when a woman called me up and said, "Dr. Ross, we have just the ideal place. The only problem is that we can only give it to you sometime in April next year." I'm always booked two years ahead of time, so that didn't bother me. I've also had so many incredible experiences that I know that I am always at the right time at the right place. So why bother about the details? Right? *(laughter from audience)*

So I didn't bother about those details. I have gotten into a lot of trouble because of that too. But anyhow I said, "Yes, fine, we will take it." And I sent a check for one thousand dollars and I forgot about it.

About a year and a half later it became time to get the plane ticket to the right island and I had to look into the details. And when I got the letter with the details on the time and the place and the date I had a total temper tantrum. I was so ugly and icky you would not believe it. I mean it lasted more than fifteen seconds. It was more like fifteen days *(laughter from audience)*.

I mean I was uglier than I remember I having been since I was two years old having temper tantrums. When your emotional quadrant overreacts, your intellectual quadrant comes to your rescue immediately. Because you could never acknowledge that this is you. So my head immediately said to me, "Those jerks! They gave me Easter week! Easter week for one of my workshops, that's impossible!" And I blamed *them* for giving me Easter week. I said to myself, "You know, I have kids at home and I'm traveling too much already, and I don't see enough of them. Next time *they* will take not only Easter away, but *they* are gonna take Christmas away. Why am I a mother at all, I never see my kids, and it's all because of *them!*"

Then I thought, "That's ridiculous. I can paint Easter eggs the weekend before, or the weekend after, so it can't be *that* terrible."

But my next line of defense was, "No, Easter will be terrible for a workshop because you don't get any Catholics. You also don't get any good Jews because it's Passover at the same time. And to have a workshop with only Protestants, I can't *stand* that." *(laughter and applause from audience)* I actually mean this very seriously because to me the beauty of my workshops is that you get every race, every creed, every age from eleven-year-old dying children to one hundred and four year old ladies. And if you have only one of a kind, you don't learn that we are all the same, that we all come from the same source and return to the same source.

I had so many excuses, but I don't want to trouble you with all of them. I was very *good*. I mean, I am a psychiatrist. I came up with *very* good excuses for being angry, you have no idea!

And nothing worked! Nothing!

⚡

I flew to Hawaii, the biggest sourpuss you have ever seen. I was even mad at my neighbors in the plane for drinking and for all sorts of stuff. I mean, I was just icky.

When I saw the place they gave me and that they assigned me to my room — it was a residential school for girls — I had another temper tantrum. I almost killed the guy who gave me the key to the room. And you have to understand why I was overreacting. I was born a triplet. It's a nightmare to be a triplet, because in those days you know, we had the same shoes, the same dresses, the same clothes, the same ribbons, the same grade cards because the teachers didn't know who was who, and so they gave us all straight C's *(laughter)*.

We even had identical night pots. And we had to pee at the same time *(laughter)* and we weren't allowed to get up from the dinner table until all three had finished. *(laughter)* So that's a big blessing I know now, and without it, no doubt I would not have made it. Because when I became a public commodity later on I was able to lecture to two or three thousand people in New York, and then sign three hundred books, then dash to Kennedy airport and just make it to the plane , and then I just *had* to go to the bathroom. I dashed in quickly and the minute I sat down, a hand came onto the door with a book, "Could you sign?" *(big laughter from audience)*

You understand why I had to be raised as a triplet! It was a preparation for my life's work.

So if you, like me, never, ever, ever had any private space, you become very tuned in to the needs of other people for *their* private space. As I walked into this room in the residential school for girls I knew that this... (I called him a crook)... this crook sent all these children home for Easter week so he could rent out the rooms and make ten thousand dollars. To make money I can understand, but what I could absolutely not forgive this guy for was that he didn't tell the girls that other people were going to live in their rooms. And any mother knows that kids don't leave certain things on the table if they know that somebody else is going to live there, right?

So it was for me like entering the sacred, private space of a child. And I really felt I couldn't use their bed or use their space. I was *angry* as can be.

Then this man made the mistake of inviting himself to my workshop. And I hated him so much I couldn't say "No." Then at dinner he stood at the end of the table where *my* group ate, and he said with a sweet smile, "Your group eats too much." And you know what I did? Me, a teacher of unconditional love? I went to every workshop participant and said, "Wouldn't you like to finish this spaghetti? How about eating the last meatballs? We don't want to leave anything. Let's finish this salad! Here is one more biscuit!" It was like an obsession. I could not leave the table as long as there was one bread crumb on the table. That was my revenge *(laughter from audience).*

But you understand, I didn't know that at the time. I was compelled, "I'm gonna show this guy that *my* group can eat." And those who ate four times, I loved them four times more than those who ate small courses. I did feel ugly but I couldn't stop it. I could not stop it as long as there was any food left on the table.

And then at night we did the drawing test. We gave the people a piece of paper and a box of Crayola. This guy very casually said, "Ten cents for a sheet of paper." This is a school! Sixty-nine cents for the *use* of a box of Crayola. Twenty-five cents for each cup of coffee. This went on all week long. Five cents, twenty-five cents, seventeen cents.

By Wednesday we sat in my workshop, and I was teaching unconditional love. But I couldn't look at this guy, because then something would have happened *(laughter from audience)*. And I was so drained you have no idea. I was exhausted trying to keep the lid on. And I didn't know what was happening.

Later, on Wednesday, I realized that I really was fantasizing that I would like to put that guy through a meat slicer *(laughter from audience)*.

By Thursday, I wanted to put iodine on every slice. *(laughter from audience)* And by Friday, I cannot remember what it was, but it was ugly too.

So Friday, at noon, I left the workshop. The workshop was a success except that *I* was ruined. I had not an inch of energy left. And normally I work seven days a week seventeen hours a day and I am very peppy.

I knew that somebody that I wasn't aware of pushed the button for Hitler within me. I had never felt so dirty, ugly, mean, nasty, like you cannot believe it. So I left that place fast before there was a homicide *(laughter from audience)*.

As I walked onto the plane I could barely make the steps. I was physically so exhausted. I first went to California, where I was to meet my friends, and then I planned to move on to Chicago hopefully to have a lovely Easter Sunday. In the plane all the way to California I was trying to think my head off, "What did this guy push, what kind of a button did he push in me?"

By the time we landed in California I suddenly became aware that I am very allergic to cheap men (*reluctant laughter from audience*). By "cheap men" I mean what you call a "penny-pincher." For I was now fully aware that if he would have been honest enough to say, "We need another two thousand dollars. We underestimated the costs," then I would have written a check for him. But the smaller the amount, the more likely I was to kill him.

I didn't know where it all came from. I had no idea.

Anybody who wants to work for Shanti Nilaya is asked to make two commitments. One is that he or she makes his house calls and his work with patients free of charge, so that he never can charge a penny. And the other commitment, which is more difficult to fulfill, is that each time he gets in touch with Hitler within, he has to work on it until he gets rid of it. Of course no one can go around preaching something and not practicing it. So now I knew I had to get rid of whatever it was.

We also have a rule that you can never ever ask anybody for something more than three times. The reason for this is that if you ask someone for something more than three times you deprive him of free choice. And it has to be *his* choice if what you ask for is to be given freely.

So now when I was going to meet my friends in California, I thought maybe I would get away with three questions about the workshop. And I came there and they said, "How was the workshop?" I said, "FINE."

"How was your workshop?" they asked again, catching my harsh tone of voice. I added two more words before the "fine" and it sounded very ugly. The third time they asked they did the worst thing that anybody can do to someone who is really ugly, and that is to be sweet with her. They put their hands on my head and in the *sweetest* way they said, "Tell us all about Easter bunnies."

And I totally exploded. I said, "Easter bunnies! You must be kidding. I'm fifty years old. I'm a physician. I'm a psychiatrist. I don't believe in Easter bunnies anymore." I made this incredible speech and at the end I said, "If you want to talk to your clients that way you know *that's* your choice, but *not* to me." And the minute I said "not to me" I started to sob and cry and I cried for eight hours.

And my whole pool of unfinished business, repressed for almost half a century, came out and out and out like an unending kind of an ocean. And as I shared the pain and the anguish and the tears and the agony and the unfairness, the memory followed, the way it always does after you have emptied your pool. As I got my emotions out — my bottled-up emotions — the memory came when I was very, very little:

My identical sister was forever on my father's lap. My other sister was forever on my mother's lap. There was no third lap left. I must have waited for God knows how long for one of them to pick me up. And as they never picked me up and never took me on their lap I began to reject *them* because I couldn't tolerate the situation otherwise. And I became a very arrogant two-year-old who said, "I don't need *you*. Don't touch me." Like I'm independent.

My love objects became bunnies. I had rabbits. And I know now that they were the only living creatures that knew me from my sister, because I fed them and they always came when I went there. I loved them beyond anything. I am sure that people could be raised by animals. I am absolutely sure of that.

My problem was that my father was a thrifty Swiss. They are all thrifty but not cheap. I hope you understand the difference *(laughter from audience)*.

Every six months he had the desire to have a roast. He could have afforded *any* roast, but *he* desired to have a rabbit roast. They were very authoritarian fifty years ago, and so he ordered me to pick one of my love objects to bring it to the butcher. And *I* had to pick — you know, like an executioner — pick a rabbit, which one's turn was it? I had to pick one of my rabbits and I had to carry him down the mountains for half an hour to the butcher. It was a tortuous thing to do. Then I had to deliver him to the butcher and after a while he always came out with a paper bag with the warm meat in it. I had to carry the meat back up the hill for half an hour and deliver it to my mother's kitchen. Later I had to sit at the dining room table and watch my family eat my beloved bunny.

Because I was an arrogant little child who covered up my insecurity and my inferiority with arrogance, I was darned careful not to let them know how much they hurt me. You understand, "If you don't love me I will also not tell you how much this hurts me." I never spoke up. I never cried. I *never* shared with a human being my pain and my anguish and my torture. I held it all inside.

It took about six months to recover and by then it was time for the next bunny.

Well, in my regressed state, when all these memories came and the tears were rolling, I became six and a half again and remembered like it was yesterday how I was kneeling down in the grass talking to my last bunny who also was my most beloved one. He was called Blackie. He was pitch black and absolutely gorgeous and very well fed with young dandelion leafs. I begged him to run away but he loved me so much he didn't move. And so eventually I had to bring him to the butcher.

I went there and handed Blackie over to him. After awhile he came out again with the paper bag and said, "damned shame you had to bring this rabbit. In a day or two she would have had little bunnies." I didn't know it was a she-bunny.

I walked home like a robot. I never had rabbits again. I never ever shared my pain and my anguish.

Today — as a psychiatrist — I understand that after that last bunny was sacrificed I had to keep the lid on not to become aware of all my tears and inner screams. Every time I met a thrifty man I had to put the lid on tighter and tighter and tighter.

Half a century later I ran into that one really thrifty man. And I almost killed him. I don't mean that symbolically speaking. *(laughter from audience; Elisabeth answers)*: No, you really have to know. If, on Friday morning, this man had asked me for another nickel he would be dead and I would be in jail *(laughter from audience)*. I am *not* meaning that as a joke. I was at the end of my rope, because my defenses were beginning to fall apart.

I thank God that we have this method of externalization used in workshops, because when I poured all this out with my friends in California it made me able to correlate and understand where my allergy to "cheap men" came from. Now I can see a hundred cheap men, and I feel that it is their problem. It's not mine any longer.

Diagnosing Black Bunnies

Out of gratitude for having been in a safe place with people who really were able to help me diagnose my unfinished business, I went back to Hawaii and we asked, in a prison, if we could be given the permission to diagnose the "black bunny" in each one of their prisoners. It took a long time before they trusted us. But eventually we were given permission to do what we wanted. Two years ago the first so-called criminal was discharged into our custody. This man now uses his life pain and anguish to help other young kids not to end up in jail.

When I shared my black bunny story in that prison, an old man asked me, "Are you not afraid to be locked up here with all these criminals?" I said "If you are a criminal I'm a criminal too." And I hope you understand that I really mean that. There is this possibility in all of us.

I told him my black bunny story. And a very, very young man who could have been my son (he didn't even have a beard yet) jumped up and said, "My God, now I know why I ended up in jail."

He shared a very brief story. He said that when he was fourteen and a half, one day when he was in school, he suddenly had this incredible urge that he had to go home. When you have this terrible urge without knowledge from your intellect, it means that it comes from the intuitive quadrant. That tells me already, for a fourteen-and-a-half-year-old boy to have that awareness, that he must have been raised with a lot of love.

And he followed his urge and dashed home. He went into the good living room. Hawaiian kids don't go into the good living room, but he walked straight in there and he saw his dad lying, half sitting on a couch, his face totally gray. He said he had such love for his father that he didn't have to scream, he didn't have to call anybody. He just sat behind him and held his dad in his arms and just loved him.

After about ten minutes he realized that his father had stopped breathing. He said that it was such an incredible moment of peace that he didn't want to go and get somebody, he just wanted to sit there for a little while.

At that moment, the paternal grandmother walked in. She had horrible problems with competition and envy. She screamed and blamed him for causing the death of her son. And he told us, "I just put the lid on. I didn't want to ruin that sacred moment." And so, he did not respond to her accusations.

Three days later, during the Hawaiian funeral, where the whole community and all the family and relatives were, this grandmother again blew her lid and blamed him in public for the death of his father. And again he said, "I just had to keep quiet. I didn't want to ruin my beloved father's funeral."

Two and a half years later he was found outside of a grocery store with a... what do you call those things?... a sawed off shotgun... holding it to the temple of a grouchy, miserable-looking old woman. He just stood there, God knows for how long. After a while he looked at her face and said, "Oh my God, what am I doing here? I don't want to hurt you." He apologized, dropped his gun and ran home.

But in a community, you know, they catch you fast. He was given twenty years in jail.

There are no bad human beings. There is a gorgeous children's book where children write letters to God. One letter says, "God didn't make junk." Do you remember it? Everybody is born perfect. If your physical quadrant is not perfect, you are gifted with a more open spiritual quadrant. Everybody is perfect. And if they are ending up not perfect, it's because they have not experienced enough love and understanding.

So I hope, over Easter, which is a marvelous time to do this kind of work, that you look at your own black bunny, and when you see somebody whom you hate, then try to understand and not judge.

(In a warm, joyful and happy voice): Thank you and have a happy Easter! *(Applause)*

PUBLISHER'S AFTERWORD

As this book goes to press, news of the terrorist bombing in Oklahoma City has barely begun to settle in. Despite what we know perfectly well — that Oklahoma is no further or closer than Bosnia or Chechnya or, for that matter, Hiroshima, Auschwitz or Dresden — it *strikes home* differently. Perhaps it's the universal human fact — the "all too human" truth — that we respond most to what comes closest to us. Elisabeth Kübler-Ross, in this regard, teaches us something bigger: that at root there's no difference between others and ourselves, between far and near, there and here. To hear her tell it, other people's suffering and dying are the major opportunity — for them and for us. If only we could learn to *be there.* And the way she puts it, there are moments when it almost sounds easy. Then comes Oklahoma City. Or the illness of a friend. Or Elisabeth Kübler-Ross's own recent experience:

> In the fall of 1994, I was out of state to receive an award for my work. I got to spend the day being remembered and cared for, instead of remembering and caring for others. My home was ready for the holidays. Boxes of completed Christmas gifts were ready to be mailed — dozens of Christmas gift stockings were wrapped for my AIDS babies, waiting to be delivered the following Monday. But it was not to be.
>
> When I returned to the Virginia Mountains I was met by a friend who tried to prevent me from returning home and finally confided to me that there was no home left. An arsonist had destroyed my home. Everything — all the handmade Christmas gifts and months of work — was incinerated to the ground. My 4,000 books and all my collections had at best been left partially intact. My pet llama was shot, and the sign leading to the center was riddled with bullet holes.
>
> I finally got the message. I was not welcome in Virginia. I told myself, "You have tried for ten years — it's time to start somewhere else." I was ready to rebuild, but my son would have no part of it. With the pretext of inviting me to a lobster dinner, he picked me up and put me on a plane to Arizona.

It is the special gift of Elisabeth Kübler-Ross that she makes ulti-mate matters and the greatest human struggles seem like some-thing that *even we* can handle, because, she tells us, the power to know the truth is inherent in us. Actually she never does say it's easy, and in fact everywhere in her writings, including this recent account, she refuses to hide her own struggle and pain. She just invites us along on the high road of what is most deeply human.

And so this book comes at a time of transition for her. Certainly the world at large has not uniformly welcomed her insights, but a vast number of people have learned directly and indirectly from her. At this moment she is in the process of receiving a series of lifetime achievement awards, which are the crest of a long mount-ing wave of recognition. And just the other day, on the occasion of one such award from the Gladys Taylor McGarey Medical Founda-tion in Scottsdale, Arizona, which is celebrating her achievement in the healing arts, she said in her acceptance remarks:

> Through my work with death and dying and AIDS pa-tients, I have gained simple insights that are important for the living as well as the dying. First, is to love; real love, that has no strings attached and, to generate this love to others. In addition, there is the incredible opportunity that physicians and healthcare providers have to be teachers, to help patients live their lives in a way that allows them to really feel whole. Physicians can help patients develop the tools to do this. It should not take a terminal illness for people to look at their own lives and realize that love and relationships are more important than jobs.

Dr. Gladys Taylor McGarey, a celebrated healer and medical pio-neer in her own right,[*] contributes a touching account of her long-time personal friend's current transition:

> On Easter morning in Arizona, Elisabeth arrived at my home for a sunrise service. She takes great delight in color-ing eggs and watching the joy on the faces of the children as they find them. As she entered, she noticed someone hid-ing the colored eggs for my grandchildren. She spontane-ously said, "They need to be hidden better, life's challenges promote growth."

Our friendship goes back many years, and I realized that Elisabeth was in the process of looking more deeply into her own personal transformation; moving from death and dying into focusing on life and living.

Although she was ready to rebuild in Virginia, her son had whisked her away to the West. Here in the pristine Arizona desert, Elisabeth is being healed by nature. It was time for her to begin another stage of her life with a new focus on healing her loss and becoming involved in a wonderful new adventure.

Responding to this new book after reading the proofs, the author wrote: "At the time that I finished *Death Is of Vital Importance* (a title, by the way, invented by the editor based on my talk in Sweden), I had been speaking with as many as 15,000 people per week for 20 years. And by this time I had come to feel that I had disseminated to the world virtually all that I had learned from my patients. Simply speaking, I had grown tired of telling the same stories again and again and I was ready for retirement from public speaking and teaching. Yet I found new pleasure in reading it again here in this book, not least of all because of the happy memories it brought back. My favorite children 'came back to life,' and along with them a part of me did too."

One thing publishers know pretty well is when an opportunity to do something important comes along. We are grateful for this one, to aid in the "dissemination" process of what in the East they could only call the Teachings. Or as Dr. McGarey puts it, "Whether it is to help in the transition of medicine, or another form of God's service, Elisabeth Kübler-Ross will continue to add her light to this world."

George Quasha
in association with Charles Stein and Susan Quasha

---

* Gladys Taylor McGarey, M.D., M.D. (H.), a pioneer in holistic medicine, natural birthing and the physician-patient partnership, has practiced medicine for fifty years and is the founder of the medical foundation that bears her name. In 1992 she was selected as one of a hundred physicians and researchers appointed to the National Institutes of Health (NIH) newly created Office of Alternative Medicine, and she is currently president of the Arizona Board of Homeopathic Examiners. She is the author of *Born to Live* and *There Will Your Heart Be Also.*

About the Author

Elisabeth Kübler-Ross is a medical doctor, psychiatrist, and world-renowned thanatologist. Her works include the classic, *On Death and Dying*, as well as *Questions and Answers on Death and Dying*, *Living with Death and Dying*, *On Children and Death*, *AIDS*, and *On Life After Death*.

About the Editor

Göran Grip, M.D. is an attending physician at the University Hospital in Uppsala, Sweden, a translator into Swedish of Elisabeth Kübler-Ross's books and other works on near-death experience and related subjects. He runs workshops in the spirit of Kübler-Ross's Life, Death and Transition workshops, and is the author of *Everything Exists*.